PARADOXES OF CATHOLICISM

PARADOXES OF CATHOLICISM

ROBERT HUGH BENSON

Roman Catholic Books

Post Office Box 2286, Fort Collins, CO 80522

NIHIL OBSTAT:
>   REMIGIUS LAFORT, D.D.
>   *CENSOR*

IMPRIMATUR:
>   ✠ JOHN CARDINAL FARLEY
>   *ARCHBISHOP OF NEW YORK*

NEW YORK, AUGUST 5, 1913

ISBN 1-929291-02-7

These sermons (which the following pages contain in a much abbreviated form) were delivered, partly in England in various places and at various times, partly in New York in the Lent of 1912, and finally, as a complete course, in the church of S. Silvestro-in-Capite, in Rome, in the Lent of 1913. Some of the ideas presented in this book have already been set out in a former volume entitled "Christ in the Church" and a few in the meditations upon the Seven Words, in another volume, but in altogether other connexions. The author thought it better, therefore, to risk repetition rather than incoherency in the present set of considerations. It is hoped that the repetitions are comparatively few.

Italics have been used for all quotations, whether verbal or substantial, from Holy Scripture and other literature.

ROBERT HUGH BENSON

HARE STREET HOUSE, BUNTINGFORD
EASTER, 1913

CONTENTS

PARADOXES OF CATHOLICISM

PARADOXES OF CATHOLICISM

INTRODUCTORY

(i) JESUS CHRIST, GOD AND MAN

I and My Father are one. — JOHN X. 30.
My Father is greater than I. — JOHN XIV. 20.

THE mysteries of the Church, a materialistic scientist
once announced to an astonished world, are child's
play compared with the mysteries of nature.[1] He
was completely wrong, of course, yet there was every
excuse for his mistake. For, as he himself tells us in
effect, he found everywhere in that created nature
which he knew so well, anomaly piled on anomaly and
paradox on paradox, and he knew no more of theology
than its simpler and more explicit statements.

We can be certain therefore — we who understand
that the mysteries of nature are, after all, within the
limited circle of created life, while the mysteries of
grace run up into the supreme Mystery of the eternal
and uncreated Life of God — we can be certain that,
if nature is mysterious and paradoxical, grace will be
incalculably more mysterious. For every paradox in

[1] Professor Huxley.

the world of matter, in whose environment our bodies
are confined, we shall find a hundred in that atmos-
phere of spirit in which our spirits breathe and move —
those spirits of ours which, themselves, paradoxically
enough, are forced to energize under material limitations.

We need look no further, then, to find these mysteries
than to that tiny mirror of the Supernatural which we
call our self, to that little thread of experience which
we name the "spiritual life." How is it, for example,
that while in one mood our religion is the lamp of our
shadowy existence, in another it is the single dark spot
upon a world of pleasure — in one mood the single
thing that makes life worth living at all, and in another
the one obstacle to our contentment? What are those
sorrowful and joyful mysteries of human life, mutually
contradictory yet together resultant (as in the Rosary
itself) in others that are glorious? Turn to that master
passion that underlies these mysteries — the passion
that is called love — and see if there be anything more
inexplicable than such an explanation. What is this
passion, then, that turns joy to sorrow and sorrow to
joy — this motive that drives a man to lose his life that
he may save it, that turns bitter to sweet and makes
the cross but a light yoke after all, that causes him to
find his centre outside his own circle, and to please
himself best by depriving himself of pleasure? What
is that power that so often fills us with delights before

we have begun to labour, and rewards our labour with the darkness of dereliction?

I. If our interior life, then, is full of paradox and apparent contradiction — and there is no soul that has made any progress that does not find it so — we should naturally expect that the Divine Life of Jesus Christ on earth, which is the central Objective Light of the World reflected in ourselves, should be full of yet more amazing anomalies. Let us examine the records of that Life and see if it be not so. And let us for that purpose begin by imagining such an examination to be made by an inquirer who has never received the Christian tradition.

(i) He begins to read, of course, with the assumption that this Life is as others and this Man as other men; and as he reads he finds a hundred corroborations of the theory. Here is one, born of a woman, hungry and thirsty by the wayside, increasing in wisdom; one who works in a carpenter's shop; rejoices and sorrows; one who has friends and enemies; who is forsaken by the one and insulted by the other — who passes, in fact, through all those experiences of human life to which mankind is subject — one who dies like other men and is laid in a grave.

Even the very marvels of that Life he seeks to explain by the marvellous humanity of its hero. He can imagine, as one such inquirer has said, how the magic of His presence was so great — the magic of His simple

yet perfect humanity — that the blind opened their
eyes to see the beauty of His face and the deaf their
ears to hear Him.

Yet, as he reads further, he begins to meet his problems. If this Man were man only, however perfect and
sublime, how is it that His sanctity appears to run by
other lines than those of other saints? Other perfect
men as they approached perfection were most conscious
of imperfection; other saints as they were nearer God
lamented their distance from Him; other teachers of
the spiritual life pointed always away from themselves
and their shortcomings to that Eternal Law to which
they too aspired. Yet with this Man all seems reversed.
He, as He stood before the world, called on men to
imitate Him; not, as other leaders have done, to avoid
His sins: this Man, so far from pointing forward and up,
pointed to Himself as the Way to the Father; so far from
adoring a Truth to which He strove, named Himself
its very incarnation; so far from describing a Life to
which He too one day hoped to rise, bade His hearers
look on Himself Who was their Life; so far from deplor-
ing to His friends the sins under which He laboured,
challenged His enemies to find within Him any sin at all.
There is an extraordinary Self-consciousness in Him
that has in it nothing of "self" as usually understood.

Then it may be, at last, that our inquirer approaches
the Gospel with a new assumption. He has been wrong,
he thinks, in his interpretation that such a Life as this

was human at all. *"Never man spake like this man."*
He echoes from the Gospel, *"What manner of man is
this that even the winds and the sea obey Him?"* How,
after all," he asks himself, "could a man be born without a human father, how rise again from the dead upon
the third day?" Or, "How even could such marvels
be related at all of one who was no more than other
men?"

So once more he begins. Here, he tells himself, is
the old fairy story come true; here is a God come down
to dwell among men; here is the solution of all his
problems. And once more he finds himself bewildered.
For how can God be weary by the wayside, labour in a
shop, and die upon a cross? How can the Eternal Word
be silent for thirty years? How can the Infinite lie in
a manger? How can the Source of Life be subject to
death?

He turns in despair, flinging himself from theory to
theory — turns to the words of Christ Himself, and
the perplexity deepens with every utterance. If Christ
be man, how can He say, *My Father and I are one?* If
Christ be God, how can He proclaim that *His Father
is greater than He?* If Christ be Man, how can He say,
Before Abraham was, I am? If Christ be God, how can
He name Himself *the Son of Man.*

(ii) Turn to the spiritual teaching of Jesus Christ,
and once more problem follows problem, and paradox,
paradox.

Here is He Who came to soothe men's sorrows and to give rest to the weary, He Who offers a sweet yoke and a light burden, telling them that no man can be His disciple who will not take up the heaviest of all burdens and follow Him uphill.　Here is one, the Physician of souls and bodies, Who *went about doing good*, Who set the example of activity in God's service, pronouncing the silent passivity of Mary as the better part that shall not be taken away from her.　Here at one moment He turns with the light of battle in His eyes, bidding His friends who have not swords to *sell their cloaks and buy them;* and at another bids those swords to be sheathed, since *His Kingdom is not of this world.*　Here is the Peacemaker, at one time pronouncing His benediction on those who make peace, and at another crying that He *came to bring not peace but a sword.* Here is He Who names as *blessed those that mourn* bidding His disciples to *rejoice and be exceeding glad.*　Was there ever such a Paradox, such perplexity, and such problems?　In His Person and His teaching alike there seems no rest and no solution—*What think ye of Christ? Whose Son is He?*

II.　(i) The Catholic teaching alone, of course, offers a key to these questions; yet it is a key that is itself, like all keys, as complicated as the wards which it alone can unlock.　Heretic after heretic has sought for simplification, and heretic after heretic has therefore come to confusion.　Christ is God, cried the Docetic;

therefore cut out from the Gospels all that speaks of
the reality of His Manhood! God cannot bleed and
suffer and die; God cannot weary; God cannot feel
the sorrows of man. Christ is Man, cries the modern
critic; therefore tear out from the Gospels His Virgin
Birth and His Resurrection! For none but a Catholic
can receive the Gospels as they were written; none but
a man who believes that Christ is both God and Man,
who is content to believe that and to bow before the
Paradox of paradoxes that we call the Incarnation, to
accept the blinding mystery that Infinite and Finite
Natures were united in one Person, that the Eternal
expresses Himself in Time, and that the Uncreated Creator united to Himself Creation — none but a Catholic,
in a word, can meet, without exception, the mysterious
phenomena of Christ's Life.

(ii) Turn now again to the mysteries of our own
limited life and, as in a far-off phantom parallel, we
begin to understand.

For we too, in our measure, have a double nature.
*As God and Man make one Christ, so soul and body make
one man:* and, as the two natures of Christ — as His
Perfect Godhead united to His Perfect Manhood —
lie at the heart of the problems which His Life presents,
so too our affinities with the clay from which our bodies
came, and with the Father of Spirits Who inbreathed
into us living souls, explain the contradictions of our
own experience.

If we were but irrational beasts, we could be as happy as the beasts; if we were but discarnate spirits that look on God, the joy of the angels would be ours. Yet if we assume either of these two truths as if it were the only truth, we come certainly to confusion. If we live as the beasts, we cannot sink to their contentment, for our immortal part will not let us be; if we neglect or dispute the rightful claims of the body, that very outraged body drags our immortal spirit down. The acceptance of the two natures of Christ alone solves the problems of the Gospel; the acceptance of the two parts of our own nature alone enables us to live as God intends. Our spiritual and physical moods, then, rise and fall as the one side or the other gains the upper hand: now our religion is a burden to the flesh, now it is the exercise in which our soul delights; now it is the one thing that makes life worth living, now the one thing that checks our enjoyment of life. These moods alternate, inevitably and irresistibly, according as we allow the balance of our parts to be disturbed and set swaying. And so, ultimately, there is reserved for us the joy neither of beasts nor of angels, but the joy of humanity. We are higher than the one, we are lower than the other, that we may be crowned by Him Who in that same Humanity sits on the Throne of God.

So much, then, for our introduction. We have seen how the Paradox of the Incarnation alone is adequate to the phenomena recorded in the Gospel — how that supreme paradox is the key to all the rest. We will proceed to see how it is also the key to other paradoxes of religion, to the difficulties which the history of Catholicism presents. For the Catholic Church is the extension of Christ's Life on earth; the Catholic Church, therefore, that strange mingling of mystery and common-sense, that union of earth and heaven, of clay and fire, can alone be understood by him who accepts her as both Divine and Human, since she is nothing else but the mystical presentment, in human terms, of Him Who, though the Infinite God and the Eternal Creator, was *found in the form of a servant,* of Him Who, *dwelling always in the Bosom of the Father,* for our sakes *came down from heaven.*

*Blessed art thou Simon Bar-jona; because flesh and blood
hath not revealed it to thee, but My Father Who is in
heaven. . . . Go behind me, satan, for thou savourest
not the things that are of God, but the things that are
of men.* — MATT. XVI. 17, 23.

WE have seen how the only reconciliation of the
paradoxes of the Gospel lies in the Catholic doctrine
of the Incarnation.   It is only to him who believes that
Jesus Christ is perfect God and perfect Man that the
Gospel record is coherent and intelligible.   The heretics
— men who for the most part either rejected or added
to the inspired record — were those who, on the one side,
accepted Christ's Divinity and rejected the proofs of
His Humanity, or accepted His Humanity and rejected
the proofs of His Divinity.   In the early ages, for the
most part, these accepted His Divinity and, rejecting
His Humanity, invented childish miracles which they
thought appropriate to a God dwelling on earth in a
phantom manhood; at the present day, rejecting His
Divinity, they reject also those miracles for which His
Divinity alone is an adequate explanation.

Now the Catholic Church is an extension of the
Incarnation.   She too (though, as we shall see, the

parallel is not perfect) has her Divine and Human Nature, which alone can account for the paradoxes of her history; and these paradoxes are either predicted by Christ — asserted, that is, as part of His spiritual teaching — or actually manifested in His own life. (We may take them as symbolised, so to speak, in those words of our Lord to St. Peter in which He first commends him as a man inspired by God and then, almost simultaneously, rebukes him as one who can rise no further than an earthly ideal at the best.)

I. (i) Just as we have already imagined a well-disposed inquirer approaching for the first time the problems of the Gospel, so let us now again imagine such a man, in whom the dawn of faith has begun, encountering the record of Catholicism.

At first all seems to him Divine. He sees, for example, how singularly unique she is, how unlike to all other human societies. Other societies depend for their very existence upon a congenial human environment; she flourishes in the most uncongenial. Other societies have their day and pass down to dissolution and corruption; she alone knows no corruption. Other dynasties rise and fall; the dynasty of Peter the Fisherman remains unmoved. Other causes wax and wane with the worldly influence which they can command; she is usually most effective when her earthly interest is at the lowest ebb.

Or again, he falls in love with her Divine beauty and

perceives even in her meanest acts a grace which he
cannot understand. He notices with wonder how she
takes human mortal things — a perishing pagan language, a debased architecture, an infant science or
philosophy — and infuses into them her own immortality. She takes the superstitions of a country-side
and, retaining their "accidents," transubstantiates them
into truth; the customs or rites of a pagan society, and
makes them the symbols of a living worship. And
into all she infuses a spirit that is all her own — a spirit
of delicate grace and beauty of which she alone has the
secret.

It is her Divinity, then, that he sees, and rightly.
But, wrongly, he draws certain one-sided conclusions. If
she is so perfect, he argues (at least subconsciously), she
can be nothing else than perfect; if she is so Divine
she can be in no sense human. Her pontiffs must all be
saints, her priests shining lights, her people stars in her
firmament. If she is Divine, her policy must be un-
erring, her acts all gracious, her lightest movements
inspired. There must be no brutality anywhere, no
self-seeking, no ambition, no instability. How should
there be, since she is Divine?

Such are his first instincts. And then, little by little,
his disillusionment begins.

For, as he studies her record more deeply, he begins
to encounter evidences of her Humanity. He reads
history, and he discovers here and there a pontiff who

but little in his moral character resembles Him Whose Vicar he is. He meets an apostate priest; he hears of some savagery committed in Christ's name; he talks with a convert who has returned complacently to the City of Confusion; there is gleefully related to him the history of a family who has kept the faith all through the period of persecution and lost it in the era of toleration. And he is shaken and dismayed. "How can these be in a Society that is Divine? I had *trusted that it had been* She *who should have redeemed Israel; and now*—!"

(ii) Another man approaches the record of Catholicism from the opposite direction. To him she is a human society and nothing more; and he finds, indeed, a thousand corroborations of his theory. He views her amazing success in the first ages of Christianity — the rapid propagation of her tenets and the growth of her influence — and sees behind these things nothing more than the fortunate circumstance of the existence of the Roman Empire. Or he notices the sudden and rapid rise of the power of the Roman pontiff and explains this by the happy chance that moved the centre of empire to the east and left in Rome an old prestige and an empty throne. He sees how the Church has profited by the divisions in Europe; how she has inherited the old Latin genius for law and order; and he finds in these things an explanation of her unity and of her claim to rule princes and kings. She is to him just human, and no more. There is not, at first sight, a phenomenon of her life for which he cannot find a human explanation. She is interesting, as a result of innumerable complicated forces; she is venerable, as the oldest coherent society in Europe; she has the advantage of Italian diplomacy; she has been shrewd, unweary, and persevering. But she is no more.

And then, as he goes deeper, he begins to encounter phenomena which do not fall so easily under his compact little theories. If she is merely human, why do not the laws of all other human societies appear to affect her too? Why is it that she alone shows no incline towards dissolution and decay? Why has not she too split up into the component parts of which she is welded? How is it that she has preserved a unity of which all earthly unities are but shadows? Or he meets with the phenomena of her sanctity and begins to perceive that the difference between the character she produces in her saints and the character of the noblest of those who do not submit to her is one of kind and not merely of degree. If she is merely mediaeval, how is it that she commands such allegiance as that which is paid to her in modern America? If she is merely European, how is it that she alone can deal with the Oriental on his own terms? If she is merely the result of temporal circumstances, how is it that her spiritual influence shows no sign of waning when the forces that helped to build her are dispersed?

His theory too, then, becomes less confident. If she is Human, why is she so evidently Divine? If she is Divine, whence comes her obvious Humanity? So years ago men asked, If Christ be God, how could He be weary by the wayside and die upon the Cross? So men ask now, If Christ be Man, how could He cast out devils and rise from the dead?

II. We come back, then, to the Catholic answer. Treat the Catholic Church as Divine only and you will stumble over her scandals, her failures, and her short-comings. Treat her as Human only and you will be silenced by her miracles, her sanctity, and her eternal resurrections.

(i) Of course the Catholic Church is Human. She consists of fallible men, and her Humanity is not even safeguarded as was that of Christ against the incursions of sin. Always, therefore, there have been scandals, and always will be. Popes may betray their trust, in all human matters; priests their flocks; laymen their faith. No man is secure. And, again, since she is human it is perfectly true that she has profited by human circumstances for the increase of her power. Undoubt-edly it was the existence of the Roman Empire, with its roads, its rapid means of transit, and its organization, that made possible the swift propagation of the Gospel in the first centuries. Undoubtedly it was the empty throne of Caesar and the prestige of Rome that developed the world's acceptance of the authority of Peter's Chair.

Undoubtedly it was the divisions of Europe that cemented the Church's unity and led men to look to a Supreme Authority that might compose their differences. There is scarcely an opening in human affairs into which she has not plunged; hardly an opportunity she has missed. Human affairs, human sins and weaknesses as well as human virtues, have all contributed to her power. So grows a tree, even in uncongenial soil. The rocks that impede the roots later become their support; the rich soil, waiting for an occupant, has been drawn up into the life of the leaves; the very winds that imperilled the young sapling have developed too its power of resistance. Yet these things do not make the tree.

(ii) For her Humanity, though it is the body in which her Divinity dwells, does not create that Divinity. Certainly human circumstances have developed her, yet what but Divine Providence ordered and developed those human circumstances? What but that same power, which indwells in the Church, dwelt without her too and caused her to take root at that time and in that place which most favored her growth? Certainly she is Human. It may well be that her rulers have contradicted one another in human matters — in science, in policy, and in discipline; but how is it, then, that they have not contradicted one another in matters that are Divine? Granted that one Pope has reversed the policy of his predecessor, then what has saved him from reversing his theology also? Certainly there have been appalling scandals, outrageous sinners, blaspheming apostates — but what of her saints?

And, above all, she gives proof of her Divinity by that very sign to which Christ Himself pointed as a proof of His own. Granted that she *dies daily* — that her cause fails in this century and in that country; that her science is discredited in this generation and her active morality in that and her ideals in a third — how comes it that she also rises daily from the dead; that her old symbols rise again from their ruins; that her virtues are acclaimed by the children of the men who renounced her; that her bells and her music sound again where once her churches and houses were laid waste?

Here, then, is the Catholic answer and it is this alone that makes sense of history, as it is Catholic doctrine which alone makes sense of the Gospel record. The answer is identical in both cases alike, and it is this —that the only explanation of the phenomena of the Gospels and of Church history is that the Life which produces them is both Human and Divine.

I
PEACE AND WAR

I

PEACE AND WAR

Blessed are the peacemakers; for they shall be called the children of God. — MATT. V. 9.

Do not think that I am come to send peace on earth; I came not to send peace but the sword. — MATT. X. 34.

WE have considered how the key to the Paradoxes of the Gospel and the key to the Paradoxes of Catholicism is one and the same — that the Life that produces them is at once Divine and Human. Let us go on to consider how this resolves those of Catholicism, especially those charged against us by our adversaries.

For we live in a day when Catholicism is no longer considered by intelligent men to be too evidently absurd to be argued with. Definite reasons are given by those who stand outside our borders for the attitude they maintain; definite accusations are made which must either be allowed or refuted.

Now those who stand without the walls of the City of Peace know nothing, it is true, of the life that its citizens lead within, nothing of the harmony and consolation that Catholicism alone can give. Yet of certain points, it may be, in the large outlines of that city against the sky, of the place it occupies in the world, of its wide effect upon human life in general, it may very well be that these detached observers may know more than the devout who dwell at peace within.   Let us, then, consider their reflections not necessarily as wholly false; it may be that they have caught glimpses which we have missed and relations which either we take too much for granted or have failed altogether to see.   It may be that these accusations will turn out to be our credentials in disguise.

I.   Every world-religion, we are told, worthy of the name has as its principal object and its chief claim to consideration its establishing or its fostering of peace among men.   Supremely this was so in the first days of Christianity.   It was this that its great prophet predicted of its work when its Divine Founder should come on earth.   Nature shall recover its lost harmony and the dissensions of men shall cease when He, the Prince of Peace, shall approach.   The very beasts shall lie down together in amity, *the lion and the lamb* and *the leopard and the kid*.   Further, it was the Message of Peace that the angels proclaimed over His cradle in Bethlehem; it was the Gift of Peace which He Himself promised to His disciples; it was the *Peace of God which passeth knowledge* to which the great Apostle commended his converts.   This then, we are told, is of the very essence of Christianity; this is the supreme benediction on the peacemakers that *they shall be called the children of God.*

Yet, when we turn to Catholicism, we are bidden to see in it not a gatherer but a scatterer, not the daughter of peace but the mother of disunion. Is there a single tormented country in Europe to-day, it is rhetorically demanded, that does not owe at least part of its misery to the claims of Catholicism? What is it but Catholicism that lies at the heart of the divided allegiance of France, of the miseries of Portugal, and of the dissensions of Italy? Look back through history and you will find the same tale everywhere. What was it that disturbed the politics of England so often from the twelfth to the fifteenth century, and tore her in two in the sixteenth, but the determined resistance of an adolescent nation to the tyranny of Rome? What lay behind the religious wars of Europe, behind the fires of Smithfield, the rack of Elizabeth, and the blood of St. Bartholomew's Day but this intolerant and intolerable religion which would come to no terms even with the most reasonable of its adversaries? It is impossible, of course, altogether to apportion blame, to say that in each several instance it was the Catholic that was the aggressor; but at least it is true to say that it was Catholic principles that were the occasion and Catholic claims the unhappy cause of all this incalculable flood of human misery.

How singularly unlike, then, we are told, is this religion

of dissension to the religion of Jesus Christ, of all these dogmatic and disciplinary claims and assertions to the meekness of the Poor Man of Nazareth! If true Christianity is anywhere in the world to-day it is not among such as these that it lies hid; rather it must be sought among the gentle humanitarians of our own and every country — men who strive for peace at all cost, men whose principal virtues are those of toleration and charity, men who, if any, have earned the beatitude of being *called the children of God.*

II. We turn to the Life of Jesus Christ from the Life of Catholicism, and at first indeed it does seem as if the contrast were justified. We cannot deny our critic's charges; every one of his historical assertions is true: it is indeed true that Catholicism has been the occasion of more bloodshedding than has any of the ambitions or jealousies of man.

And it is, further, true that Jesus Christ pronounced this benediction; that He bade His followers seek after peace, and that He commended them, in the very climax of His exaltation, to the Peace which He alone could bestow.

Yet, when we look closer, the case is not so simple. For, first, what was, as a matter of fact, the direct immediate effect of the Life and Personality of Jesus Christ upon the society in which He lived but this very dissension, this very bloodshedding and misery that are charged against His Church? It was precisely on this account that He was given into the hands of Pilate. *He stirreth up the people. He makes Himself a King. He* is a contentious demagogue, a disloyal citizen, a danger to the Roman Peace.

And indeed there seem to have been excuses for these charges. It was not the language of a modern "humanitarian," of the modern tolerant "Christian," that fell from the Divine Lips of Jesus Christ. *Go and tell that fox*, He cries of the ruler of His people. *O you whited sepulchres full of dead men's bones! You vipers! You hypocrites!* This is the language He uses to the representatives of Israel's religion. Is this the kind of talk that we hear from modern leaders of religious thought? Would such language as this be tolerated for a moment from the humanitarian Christian pulpits of to-day? Is it possible to imagine more inflammatory speech, more "unchristian sentiments," as they would be called to-day, than those words uttered by none other but the Divine Founder of Christianity? What of that amazing scene when He threw the furniture about the temple courts?

And as for the effect of such words and methods, our Lord Himself is quite explicit. "Make no mistake," He cries to the modern humanitarian who claims alone to represent Him. "Make no mistake. I am *not come to bring peace* at any price; there are worse things than war and bloodshed. I am *come to bring not peace but a sword*. I am come to *divide families*, not to unite them;

to rend kingdoms, not to knit them up; I am come *to set mother against daughter and daughter against mother;* I am come not to establish universal toleration, but universal Truth."

What, then, is the reconciliation of the Paradox? In what sense can it be possible that the effect of the Personality of the Prince of Peace, and therefore the effect of His Church, in spite of their claims to be the friends of peace, should be *not peace, but the sword?*

III. Now (1) the Catholic Church is a Human Society. She is constituted, that is to say, of human beings; she depends, humanly speaking, upon human circumstances; she can be assaulted, weakened, and disarmed by human enemies. She dwells in the midst of human society, and it is with human society that she has to deal.

Now if she were not human — if she were merely a Divine Society, a far-off city in the heavens, a future distant ideal to which human society is approximating, there would be no conflict at all. She would never meet in a face-to-face shock the passions and antagonisms of men; she could suppress, now and again, her Counsels of Perfection, her calls to a higher life, if it were not that these are vital and present principles which she is bound to propagate among men.

And again, if she were merely human, there would be no conflict. If she were merely ascended from below, merely the result of the finest religious thought of the world, the high-water mark of spiritual attainment, again she could compromise, could suppress, could be silent.

But she is both human and divine, and therefore her warfare is certain and inevitable. For she dwells in the midst of the kingdoms of this world, and these are constituted, at any rate at the present day, on wholly human bases. Statesmen and kings, at the present day, do not found their policies upon supernatural considerations; their object is to govern their subjects, to promote the peace and union of their subjects, to make war, if need be, on behalf of the peace of their subjects, wholly on natural grounds. Commerce, finance, agriculture, education in the things of this world, science, art, exploration — human activities generally — these, in their purely natural aspect, are the objects of nearly all modern statesmanship. Our rulers are professedly, in their public capacity, neither for religion nor against it; religion is a private matter for the individual, and governments stand aside — or at any rate profess to do so.

And it is in this kind of world, in this fashion of human society, that the Catholic Church, in virtue of her humanity, is bound to dwell. She too is a kingdom, though not of this world, yet in it.

(2) For she is also Divine. Her message contains, that is to say, a number of supernatural principles revealed to her by God; she is supernaturally consti-

tuted; she rests on a supernatural basis; she is not organized as if this world were all. On the contrary she puts the kingdom of God definitely first and the kingdoms of the world definitely second; the Peace of God first and the harmony of men second.

Therefore she is bound, when her supernatural principles clash with human natural principles, to be the occasion of disunion. Her marriage laws, as a single example, are at conflict with the marriage laws of the majority of modern States. It is of no use to tell her to modify these principles; it would be to tell her to cease to be supernatural, to cease to be herself. How can she modify what she believes to be her Divine Message?

Again, since she is organized on a supernatural basis, there are supernatural elements in her own constitution which she can no more modify than her dogmas. Recently, in France, she was offered the *kingdom of this world* if she would do so; it was proposed to her that she actually retain her own wealth, her churches and her houses, and yield up her principle of spiritual appeal to the Vicar of Christ. If she had been but human, how evident would have been her duty! · How inevitable that she should modify her constitution in accordance with human ideas and preserve her property intact! And how entirely impossible such a bargain must be for a Society that is divine as well as human!

Take courage then! We desire peace above all things — that is to say, the Peace of God, not *that peace which the world*, since it *can give* it, can also *take away;* not that peace which depends on the harmony of nature with nature, but of nature with grace.

Yet, so long as the world is divided in allegiance; so long as the world, or a country, or a family, or even an individual soul bases itself upon natural principles divorced from divine, so long to that world, that country, that family, and that human heart will the supernatural religion of Catholicism bring *not peace, but a sword.* And it will do so to the end, up to the final world-shattering catastrophe of Armageddon itself.

"I come," cries the Rider on the White Horse, "to bring Peace indeed, but a peace of which the world cannot even dream; a peace built upon the eternal foundations of God Himself, not upon the shifting sands of human agreement. And until that Vision dawns there must be war; until God's Peace descends indeed and is accepted, till then *My Garments must be splashed in blood* and from My Mouth comes forth *not peace, but a two-edged sword.*"

II

WEALTH AND POVERTY

II

WEALTH AND POVERTY

Make to yourselves friends of the Mammon of iniquity.
You cannot serve God and Mammon. — LUKE XVI. 9, 13.

WE have seen how the Church of the Prince of Peace must continually be the centre of war. Let us go on to consider how, as a Human Society dwelling in this world, she must continually have her eyes fixed upon the next, and how, as a Divine Society, she must be open to the charge of worldliness.

I. (i) The charge is a very common one: "Look at the extraordinary wealth and splendour that this Church of the Poor Man of Nazareth constantly gathers around her and ask yourself how she can dare to claim to represent Him! Go through Holy Rome and see how the richest and most elaborate buildings bear over their gateways the heraldic emblems of Christ's Vicar! Go through any country which has not risen in disgust and cast off the sham that calls herself 'Christ's Church' and you will find that no worldly official is so splendid as these heavenly delegates of Jesus Christ, no palaces more glorious than those in which they dwell who pretend to preach Him who *had not where to lay His head!*

"Above all, turn from that simple poverty-stricken figure that the Gospels present to us, to the man who claims to be His Vicegerent on earth. See him go, crowned three times over, on a throne borne on men's shoulders, with the silver trumpets shrilling before him and the ostrich fans coming on behind, and you will understand why the world cannot take the Church seriously. Look at the court that is about him, all purple and scarlet, and set by that the little band of weather-beaten fishermen!

"No; if this Church were truly of Christ, she would imitate Him better. It was His supreme mission to point to *things that are above;* to lift men's thoughts above dross and gold and jewels and worldly influence and high places and power; to point to *a Heavenly Jerusalem, not made with hands;* to comfort the sorrowful with a vision of future peace, not to dabble with temporal matters; to speak of grace and heaven and things to come, and *to let the dead bury their dead!* The best we can do for her, then, is to disembarrass her of her riches; to turn her temporal possessions to frankly temporal ends; to release her from the slavery of her own ambition into the *liberty of the poor and the children of God!*"

(ii) In a word, then, the Church is too worldly to be the Church of Christ! *You cannot serve God and Mammon.* Yet in another mood our critic will tell us that we are too otherworldly to be the Church of Christ. "The chief charge I have against Catholicism," says such a man, "is that the Church is too unpractical. If she were truly the Church of Jesus Christ, she would surely imitate Him better in that which, after all, was the mark of His highest Divinity — namely in His Humanity towards men. Christ did not come into the world to preach metaphysics and talk forever of a heaven that is to come; He came rather to attend to men's simplest needs, *to feed the hungry, to clothe the naked*, to reform society on better lines. It was not by His dogma that He won men's hearts; it was by His simple, natural sympathy with their common needs. He came, in a word, to make the best of this world, to use the elements that lay ready to His hand, to sanctify all the plain things of earth with which He came in contact.

"These otherworldly Catholics, then, are too much apart from common life and common needs. Their dogmas and their aspirations and their metaphysics are useless to a world which wants bread. Let them act more and dream less! Let them show, for example, by the prosperity of Catholic countries that Catholicism is practical and not a vision. Let them preach less and philanthropize more. Let them show that they have the key to this world's progress, and perhaps we will listen more patiently to their claim to hold the key to the world that is to come!"

But, surely, this is a little hard upon Catholics! When we make ourselves at home in this world, we are informed that Jesus Christ *had not where to lay His Head.*

When we preach the world that is to come, we are re-
minded that Jesus Christ after all came down from that
world into this to make it better. When we build a
comfortable church, we are told that we are too luxurious.
When we build an uncomfortable one we are asked how
we expect to do any good unless we are practical.

II. Now, of course, both these charges were also
objected against our Blessed Lord. For He too had His
double activities. It is true that there were times when
He gave men earthly bread; it is also true that He
offered them heavenly bread. There were times when
He cared for men's bodies; there were other times when
He bade them sacrifice all that makes bodily life worth
living; times when He sat at meat in the house of a
rich man, and times when He starved, voluntarily, in
the desert.

And the world found Him wrong whichever He did.
He was too worldly when He healed men on the Sabbath;
for is not the Law of God of more value than a man's
bodily ease? Why can He not wait till to-morrow?
He was too worldly when He allowed His disciples to
rub corn in their hands; for does not the Law of God
forbid a man to make bread on the Sabbath? He was
too worldly, too unpractical, too sense-loving when He
permitted the precious ointment to be spilled on His
feet; *for might not this ointment have been sold for much
and given to the poor?* Is not spirituality enough, and
the incense of adoration?

And He was too otherworldly when He preached the Sermon on the Mount. What is the use of saying, *Blessed are the Meek*, when the whole world knows that "Blessed are the Self-Assertive"? He was too otherworldly when He spoke of Heavenly Bread. What is the use of speaking of Heavenly Bread when it is earthly food that men need first of all? He was too otherworldly when He remained in the country on the feast day. *If He be the Christ*, let Him be practical and say so!

It was, in fact, on these very two charges that He was arraigned for death. He was too worldly for Pilate, in that He was Son of Man and therefore a rival to Caesar; and too otherworldly for Caiphas, since *He made Himself Son of God* and therefore a rival to Jehovah.

III. The solution, then, of this Catholic Paradox is very simple. (i) First, the Church is a Heavenly Society come down from above — heavenly in her origin and her birth. She is the *kingdom of God*, first and foremost, and exists for His glory solely and entirely. She seeks, then, first the extension of His kingdom; and compared with this, nothing is of any value in her eyes. Never, then, must she sacrifice God to Mammon; never hesitate for one instant if the choice lies between them. For she considers that eternity is greater than time and the soul of man of more value than his body. The sacraments therefore, in her eyes, come before an adequate tram-service; and that a man's soul should be in grace is, to her, of more importance than that his body should be in health — if the choice is between them. She prefers, therefore, the priest to the doctor, if there is not time for both, and Holy Communion to a good breakfast.

Therefore, of course, she appears too otherworldly to the stockbroker and the provincial mayor, since she actually places the things of God before the things of man and "seeks first His Kingdom."

(ii) "And all these things shall be added" to her. For she is Human also, in that she dwells in this world where God has placed her, and uses therefore the things with which He has surrounded her. To say that she is supernatural is not to deny her humanity any more than to assert that man has an immortal soul is to exclude the truth that he also has a body. It is this Body of hers, then — this humanity of hers which enshrines her Divinity — that claims and uses earthly things; it is this Body that *dwells in houses made with hands* and that claims too, in honour to herself and her Bridegroom, that, so long as her spirituality is not tarnished, these houses shall be as splendid as art can make them. For she is not a Puritan nor a Manichee; she does not say that any single thing which God has made can conceivably be of itself evil, however grievously it may have been abused; on the contrary, she has His own authority for saying that *all is very good.*

She uses, then, every earthly beauty that the world will yield to her, to honour her own Majesty. It may

be right to set diamonds round the neck of a woman,
but it is certainly right to set them round the Chalice
of the Blood of God. If an earthly king wears vestments
of cloth of gold, must not a heavenly King yet more
wear them? If music is used by the world to destroy
men's souls, may not she use it to save their souls? If
a marble palace is fit for the President of the French
Republic, by what right do men withhold it from the
King of kings?

But the world does withhold its wealth sometimes?
Very well then, she can serve God without it, in spite of
her rights. If men whine and cringe, or bully and shout,
for the jewels with which their forefathers honoured God,
she will fling them back again down her altar stairs and
worship God in a barn or a catacomb without them.
For, though she does not *serve God and Mammon*, she yet
makes to herself friends of the Mammon of iniquity. Though
she does not and never can serve God and Mammon,
she will and can, when the world permits it, make Mammon serve her. For the Church is the Majesty of God
dwelling on earth. She is there, in herself, utterly inde-
pendent of her reception. If it is *her own* to whom *she
comes, and her own do not receive her*, they are none the
less hers by every right. For, though she will use every
earthly thing to her honour, though she considers no
ointment wasted, however precious, that is spilled by
love over her feet, yet her essential glory does not lie
in these things. She is *all glorious within*, whether or

not her *vesture is of gold*, for she is a *King's Daughter*.
She is, essentially, as glorious in the Catacombs as in the
Roman basilicas; as lovely in the barefooted friar as
in the robed and sceptred Vicar of Christ; as majestic
in Christ naked on the Cross as in Christ ascended and
enthroned in heaven.

Yet, since she is His Majesty on earth, she has a right
to all that earth can give. All *the beasts of the field are
hers, and the cattle on a thousand hills*, all the stars of
heaven and the jewels of earth; all the things in the
world are hers by Divine right.

All things are hers, for she is Christ's. Yet, never-
theless, *she will suffer the loss of all things* sooner than
lose Him.

III

SANCTITY AND SIN

SANCTITY AND SIN

Holy, Holy, Holy! — IS. VI. 3.
Christ Jesus came into this world to save sinners.
I TIM. I. 15.

A VERY different pair of charges — and far more vital
— than those more or less economic accusations of
worldliness and otherworldliness which we have just
considered, concern the standards of goodness preached
by the Church and her own alleged incapacity to live up
to them. These may be briefly summed up by saying
that one-half the world considers the Church too holy
for human life, and the other half, not holy enough.
We may name these critics, respectively, the Pagan and
the Puritan.

I. It is the Pagan who charges her with excessive
Holiness.

"You Catholics," he tells us, "are far too hard on sin
and not nearly indulgent enough towards poor human
nature. Let me take as an instance the sins of the
flesh. Now here is a set of desires implanted by God or
Nature (as you choose to name the Power behind life)

for wise and indeed essential purposes. These desires
are probably the very fiercest known to man and certainly
the most alluring; and human nature is, as we know, an
extraordinarily inconsistent and vacillating thing. Now
I am aware that the abuse of these passions leads to
disaster and that Nature has her inexorable laws and
penalties; but you Catholics add a new horror to life
by an absurd and irrational insistence on the offence
that this abuse causes before God. For not only do you
fiercely denounce the "acts of sin," as you name them,
but you presume to go deeper still to the very desire
itself, as it would seem. You are unpractical and cruel
enough to say that the very thought of sin deliberately
entertained can cut off the soul that indulges in it from
the favour of God.

"Or, to go further, consider the impossible ideals
which you hold up with regard to matrimony. These
ideals have a certain beauty of their own to persons who
can embrace them; they may perhaps be, to use a
Catholic phrase, Counsels of Perfection; but it is merely
ludicrous to insist upon them as rules of conduct for all
mankind. Human Nature is human nature. You cannot bind the many by the dreams of the few.

"Or, to take a wider view altogether, consider the
general standards you hold up to us in the lives of your
saints. These saints appear to the ordinary common-
place man as simply not admirable at all. It does not
seem to us admirable that St. Aloysius should scarcely

lift his eyes from the ground, or that St. Teresa should shut herself up in a cell, or that St. Francis should scourge himself with briers for fear of committing sin. That kind of attitude is too fantastically fastidious altogether. You Catholics seem to aim at a standard that is simply not desirable; both your ends and your methods are equally inhuman and equally unsuitable for the world we have to live in. True religion is surely something far more sensible than this; true religion should not strain and strive after the impossible, should not seek to improve human nature by a process of mutilation. You have excellent aims in some respects and excellent methods in others, but in supreme demands you go beyond the mark altogether. We Pagans neither agree with your morality nor admire those whom you claim as your successes. If you were less holy and more natural, less idealistic and more practical, you would be of a greater service to the world which you desire to help. Religion should be a sturdy, virile growth; not the delicate hot-house blossom which you make it."

The second charge comes from the Puritan. "Catholicism is not holy enough to be the Church of Jesus Christ; for see how terribly easy she is to those who outrage and *crucify Him afresh!* Perhaps it may not be true after all, as we used to think, that the Catholic priest actually gives leave to his penitents to commit sin; but the extraordinary ease with which absolution is given comes very nearly to the same thing. So far from this Church having elevated the human race, she has actually lowered its standards by her attitude towards those of her children who disobey God's Laws.

"And consider what some of these children of hers have been! Are there any criminals in history so monumental as Catholic criminals? Have any men ever fallen so low as, let us say, the Borgia family of the Middle Ages, as Gilles de Rais and a score of others, as men and women who were perhaps in their faith 'good Catholics' enough, yet in their lives a mere disgrace to humanity? Look at the Latin countries with their passionate records of crime, at the sexual immorality of France or Spain; the turbulence and thriftlessness of Ireland, the ignorant brutality of Catholic England. Are there any other denominations of Christendom that exhibit such deplorable specimens as the runaway nuns, the apostate priests, the vicious Popes of Catholicism? How is it that tales are told of the iniquities of Catholicism such as are told of no other of the sects of Christendom? Allow for all the exaggeration you like, all the prejudice of historians, all the spitefulness of enemies, yet there surely remains sufficient Catholic criminality to show that at the best the Church is no better than any other religious body, and at the worst, infinitely worse. The Catholic Church, then, is not holy enough to be the Church of Jesus Christ."

II. When we turn to the Gospels we find that these two charges are, as a matter of fact, precisely among those which were brought against our Divine Lord.

First, undoubtedly, He was hated for His Holiness. Who can doubt that the terrific standard of morality which He preached — the Catholic preaching of which also is one of the charges of the Pagan — was a principal cause of His rejection. For it was He, after all, who first proclaimed that the laws of God bind not only action but thought; it was He who first pronounced that man to be a murderer and an adulterer who in his heart willed these sins; it was He who summed up the standard of Christianity as a standard of perfection, *Be you perfect, as your Father in Heaven is perfect;* who bade men aspire to be as good as God!

It was His Holiness, then, that first drew on Him the hostility of the world — that radiant white-hot sanctity in which His Sacred Humanity went clothed. *Which of you convinceth me of sin? . . . Let him that is without sin amongst you cast the first stone at her!* These were words that pierced the smooth formalism of the Scribe and the Pharisee and awoke an undying hatred. It was this, surely, that led up irresistibly to the final rejection of Him at the bar of Pilate and the choice of Barabbas in His place. "*Not this man!* not this piece of stainless Perfection! Not this Sanctity that reveals all hearts, *but Barabbas*, that comfortable sinner so like ourselves! This robber in whose company we feel at ease! This murderer whose life, at any rate, is in no reproachful

contrast to our own!" Jesus Christ was found too holy
for the world.

But He was found, too, not holy enough. And it is
this explicit charge that is brought against Him again
and again. It was dreadful to those keepers of the Law
that this Preacher of Righteousness should sit with
publicans and sinners; that this Prophet should allow
such a woman as Magdalen to touch Him. If this man
were indeed a Prophet, He could not bear the contact
of sinners; if He were indeed zealous for God's Kingdom,
He could not suffer the presence of so many who were
its enemies. Yet He sits there at Zacchaeus' table, silent
and smiling, instead of crying on the roof to fall in; He
calls Matthew from the tax-office instead of blasting him
and it together; He handles the leper whom God's own
Law pronounces unclean.

III. These, then, are the charges brought against
the disciples of Christ, as against the Master, and it is
undeniable that there is truth in them both.

It is true that the Catholic Church preaches a morality
that is utterly beyond the reach of human nature left
to itself; that her standards are standards of perfection,
and that she prefers even the lowest rung of the supernatural ladder to the highest rung of the natural.

And it is also true, without doubt, that the fallen or
the unfaithful Catholic is an infinitely more degraded
member of humanity than the fallen Pagan or Protestant; that the monumental criminals of history are

Catholic criminals, and that the monsters of the world—
Henry VIII for example, sacrilegious, murderer, and
adulterer; Martin Luther, whose printed table-talk is
unfit for any respectable house; Queen Elizabeth, per-
jurer, tyrant, and unchaste—were persons who had had
all that the Catholic Church could give them: the
standards of her teaching, the guidance of her discipline,
and the grace of her sacraments. What, then, is the
reconciliation of this Paradox?

(1) First the Catholic Church is Divine. She dwells,
that is to say, in heavenly places; she looks always upon
the Face of God; she holds enshrined in her heart the
Sacred Humanity of Jesus Christ and the stainless perfection of that Immaculate Mother from whom that
Humanity was drawn. How is it conceivable, then, that
she should be content with any standard short of perfection? If she were a Society evolved from below — a
merely human Society that is to say — she could never
advance beyond those standards to which in the past
her noblest children have climbed. But since there
dwells in her the Supernatural — since Mary was en-
dowed from on high with a gift to which no human being
could ascend, since the Sun of Justice Himself came down
from the heavens to lead a human life under human
terms — how can she ever again be content with anything short of that height from which these came?

(2) But she is also human, dwelling herself in the
midst of humanity, placed here in the world for the

express object of gathering into herself and of sanctifying
by her graces that very world which has fallen from
God.   These outcasts and these sinners are the very
material on which she has to work; these waste pro-
ducts of human life, these marred types and specimens
of humanity have no hope at all except in her.

For, first, she desires if she can — and she has often
been able — actually to raise these, first to sanctity and
then to her own altars; it is for her and her only to *raise
the poor from the dunghill and to set them with the princes.*
She sets before the Magdalen and the thief, then, nothing
less but her own standard of perfection.

Yet though in one sense she is satisfied with nothing
lower than this, in another sense she is satisfied with
almost infinitely nothing.   If she can but bring the
sinner within the very edge of grace; if she can but
draw from the dying murderer one cry of contrition; if
she can but turn his eyes with one look of love to the
crucifix, her labours are a thousand times repaid; for,
if she has not brought him to the head of sanctity, she
has at least brought him to its foot and set him there
beneath that ladder of the supernatural which reaches
from hell to heaven.

For she alone has this power.   She alone is so utterly
confident in the presence of the sinner because she alone
has the secret of his cure.   There in her confessional is
the Blood of Christ that can make his soul clean again,
and in her Tabernacle the Body of Christ that will

be his food of eternal life. She alone dares be his
friend because she alone can be his Saviour. If, then,
her saints are one sign of her identity, no less are her
sinners another.

For not only is she the Majesty of God dwelling on
earth, she is also His Love; and therefore its limitations,
and they only, are hers. That Sun of mercy that shines
and that Rain of charity that streams, *on just and unjust
alike*, are the very Sun and Rain that give her life. *If I
go up to Heaven she is there*, enthroned in Christ, on the
Right Hand of God; *if I go down to Hell she is there
also*, drawing back souls from the brink from which she
alone can rescue them. For she is that very ladder
which Jacob saw so long ago, that staircase planted here
in the blood and the slime of earth, rising there into the
stainless Light of the Lamb. Holiness and unholiness
are both alike hers and she is ashamed of neither — the
holiness of her own Divinity which is Christ's and the
unholiness of those outcast members of her Humanity
to whom she ministers.

By her power, then, which again is Christ's, the
Magdalen becomes the Penitent; the thief the first of
the redeemed; and Peter, the yielding sand of humanity,
the *Rock on which Herself is built*.

IV

JOY AND SORROW

IV

JOY AND SORROW

Rejoice and be exceeding glad. . . . Blessed are they that mourn. — MATT. V. 12, 5.

THE Catholic Church, as has been seen, is always too "extreme" for the world. She is content with nothing but a Divine Peace, and in its cause is the occasion of bloodier wars than any waged from merely human motives. She is not content with mere goodness, but urges always Sanctity upon her children; yet simultaneously tolerates sinners whom even the world casts out. Let us consider now how, in fulfilling these two apparently mutually contradictory precepts of our Lord,. to rejoice and to mourn, once more she appears to the world extravagant in both directions at once.

I. It is a common charge against her that she rejoices too exceedingly; is arrogant, confident, and optimistic where she ought to be quiet, subdued, and tender.

"This world," exclaims her critic, "is on the whole a very sad and uncertain place. There is no silver lining that has not a cloud before it; there is no hope that may not, after all, be disappointed. Any religion, then, that claims to be adequate to human nature must always have something of sadness and even hesitancy about it. Religion must walk softly all her days if she is to walk hand in hand with experience. Death is certain; is life as certain? The function of religion, then, is certainly to help to lighten this darkness, yet not by too great a blaze of light. She may hope and aspire and guess and hint; in fact, that is her duty. But she must not proclaim and denounce and command. She must be suggestive rather than exhaustive; tender rather than virile; hopeful rather than positive; experimental rather than dogmatic.

"Now Catholicism is too noisy and confident altogether. See a Catholic liturgical function on some high day! Was there ever anything more arrogant? What has this blaze of colour, this shouting of voices, this blowing of trumpets to do with the soft half-lights of the world and the mystery of the darkness from which we came and to which we return? What has this clearcut dogma to do with the gentle guesses of philosophy, this optimism with the uncertainty of life and the future — above all, what sympathy has this preposterous exultation with the misery of the world?

"And how unlike, too, all this is to the spirit of the Man of Sorrows! We read that *Jesus wept*, but never that He laughed. His was a sad life, from the dark stable of Bethlehem to the darker hill of Calvary. He was what He was because He knew what sorrow meant;

it was in His sorrows that He has touched the heart of humanity. '*Blessed*,' he says, '*are those that mourn.*' Blessed are they that expect nothing, for they shall not be disappointed."

In another mood, however, our critic will find fault with our sadness.

"Why is not the religion of you Catholics more in accord with the happy world in which we live? Surely the supreme function of religion is to hearten and encourage and lay stress on the bright side of life! It should be brief, bright, and brotherly. For, after all, this is a lovely world and full of gaiety. It is true that it has its shadows, yet there can be no shadows without a sun; there is death, but see how life continually springs again from the grave. Since all things, therefore, work together for good; since God has taken pains to make the world so sweet, it is but a poor compliment to the Creator to treat it as a vale of misery. Let us, then, make the best of things and forget the worst. Let us leave the things that are behind and press forward to the things that are before. Let us insist that the world is white with a few black spots upon it, be optimistic, happy, and confident.

"You Catholics, however, are but a poor-spirited, miserable race. While other denominations are, little by little, eliminating melancholy, you are insisting upon it. While the rest of us are agreeing that Hell is but a bogy, and sin a mistake, and suffering no more than remedial, you Catholics are still insisting upon their reality — that Hell is eternal, that sin is the deliberate opposition of the human will to the Divine, and that suffering therefore is judicial. Sin, Penance, Sacrifice, Purgatory, and Hell — these are the old nightmares of dogma; and their fruits are tears, pain, and terror. What is wrong with Catholicism, then, is its gloom and its sorrow; for this is surely not the Christianity of Christ as we are now learning to understand it. Christ, rightly understood, is the Man of Joy, not of Grief. He is more characteristic of Himself, so to speak, as the smiling shepherd of Galilee, surrounded by His sheep; as the lover of children and flowers and birds; as the Preacher of Life and Resurrection — He is more characteristic of Himself as crowned, ascended, and glorified, than as the blood-stained martyr of the Cross whom you set above your altars. *Rejoice, then, and be exceeding glad*, and you will please Him best."

Once more, then, we appear to be in the wrong, to whatever side we turn. The happy red-faced monk with his barrel of beer is a caricature of our joy. Can this, it is asked, be a follower of the Man of Sorrows? And the long-faced ascetic with his eyes turned up to heaven is the world's conception of our sorrow. Catholic joy and Catholic sorrow are alike too ardent and extreme for a world that delights in moderation in both sorrow and joy — a little melancholy, but not too much; a little cheerfulness, but not excessive.

II. First, then, it is interesting to remember that these charges are not now being made against us for the first time. In the days even of the Roman Empire they were thought to be signs of Christian inhumanity. "These Christians," it was said, "must surely be bewitched. See how they laugh at the rack and the whip and go to the arena as to a bridal bed! See how Lawrence jests upon his gridiron." And yet again, "They must be bewitched, because of their morbidity and their love of darkness, the enemies of joy and human mirth and common pleasure. In either case they are not true men at all." Their extravagance of joy when others would be weeping, and their extravagance of sorrow when all the world is glad — these are the very signs to which their enemies appealed as proofs that a power other than that of this world was inspiring them, as proofs that they could not be the simple friends of the human race that they dared to pretend.

It is even more interesting to remember that our Divine Lord Himself calls attention to these charges. *"The Son of Man comes eating and drinking.* The Son of Man sits at the wedding feast at Cana and at meat in the rich man's house and you say, *Behold a glutton and a winebibber!* The Son of Man comes rejoicing and you bid Him to be sad. And *John the Baptist came neither eating nor drinking.* John the Baptist comes from the desert, an ascetic with his camel-hair about him and words of penance and wrath in his mouth, and you say, *He hath a devil. . . . We have piped unto you and you have not danced.* We have played at weddings like children in a market-place, and you have told us to be quiet and think about our sins. *We have mourned unto you*, we have asked you to play at funerals instead, and you have told us that it was morbid to think about death. *We have mourned and you would not lament.*"

III. The fact is, of course, that both joy and sorrow must be an element in all religion, since joy and sorrow together make up experience. The world is neither white with black spots nor black with white spots; it is black and white. It is quite as true that autumn follows summer as that spring follows winter. It is no less true that life arises out of death than that death follows life.

Religion then cannot, if it is to be adequate to experience, be a passionless thing. On the contrary it must be passionate, since human nature is passionate too; and it must be a great deal more passionate. It must not moderate grief, but deepen it; not banish joy, but exalt it. It must weep — and bitterer tears than any that the world can shed — with them that weep; and rejoice too — with *a joy which no man can take away* — with them that rejoice. It must sink deeper and rise higher, it must feel more acutely, it must agonize and triumph more abundantly, if it truly comes from God and is to minister to men, since His thoughts are higher than ours and His Love more burning.

For so did Christ live on earth. At one hour He *rejoiced greatly in spirit* so that those that watched Him were astonished; at another He sweated blood for anguish. In one hour He is exalted high on the blazing Mount of Transfiguration; in another He is plunged deeper than any human heart can fathom in the low-lying garden of Gethsemane. *Behold and see if there be any sorrow like to My Sorrow.*

III. For, again, the Church, like her Lord, is both Divine and Human.

She is Divine and therefore she rejoices — so filled with the New Wine of the Kingdom of her Father that men stare at her in contempt.

It is true enough that the world is unhappy; that hearts are broken; that families, countries, and centuries are laid waste by sin. Yet since the Church is Divine, she knows, not merely guesses or hopes or desires, but *knows*, that *although all things come to an end, God's commandment is exceeding broad.* Years ago, she knows — and therefore not all the criticism in the world can shake her — that her Lord came down from heaven, was born, died, rose, and ascended, and that He reigns in unconquerable power. She knows that He will return again and take the kingdom and reign; she knows, because she is Divine, that in every tabernacle of hers on earth the Lord of Joy lies hidden; that Mary intercedes; that the saints are with God; that *the Blood of Jesus Christ cleanseth from all sin.* Look round her earthly buildings, then, and there are the symbols and images of these things. There is the merry light before her altar; there are the saints stiff with gold and gems; there is Mary, "Cause of our Joy," radiant, with her radiant Child in her arms. If she were but human, she would dare but to shadow these things forth — shadows of her own desires; she would whisper her creed; murmur her prayers; darken her windows. But she is Divine and has herself come down from heaven; so she does not guess, or think, or hope — she knows.

But she is human too and dwells in the midst of a human race that does not know and therefore will not wholly take her at her word, and the very height of her exaltation must also be, then, the measure of her despair. The fact that she knows so certainly intensifies a thousandfold her human sorrow, as she, who has *come that they may have life*, sees how *they will not come* to her and find it, as she sees how long the triumph which is certain is yet delayed through their faithlessness. "*If thou hadst known*," she cries in the heart-broken words of Jesus Himself over Jerusalem, "*if thou hadst but known the things that belong to thy peace! Behold and see, then, if there be any sorrow like to mine*, if there be any grief so profound and so piercing as mine, who hold the Keys of Heaven and watch men turn away from the Door."

So, then, in church after church stand symbolic groups of statuary, representing joy and tragedy, compared with which Venus and Adonis are but childish and half-civilized images — Mary as triumphant Queen, with the gold-crowned Child in her arms, and Mary the tormented Mother, with her dead Son across her knees. For she who is both Divine and Human alone understands what it is that Humanity has done to Divinity.

Is it any wonder, then, that the world thinks her extravagant in both directions at once; that the world turns away on Good Friday from the unutterable depths of her sorrow, and on Easter Day from the unscalable heights of her joy, calling the one morbid and the other hysterical? For what does the world know of such passions as these? What, after all, can the sensualist know of joy, or the ruined financier of sorrow? And what can the moderate, self-controlled, self-respecting man of the world know of either?

Lastly, then, in the Paradox of Love, the Church holds both these passions, at full blast, both at once. As human love turns joy into pain and suffers in the midst of ecstasy, so Divine Love turns pain into joy and exults and reigns upon the Cross. For the Church is more than the Majesty of God reigning on earth, more than the passionless love of the Eternal; she is the Very Sacred Heart of Christ Himself, the Eternal united with Man, and both suffering and rejoicing through that union. It is His bliss which she at once experiences and extends, in virtue of her identity with Him; and in the midst of a fallen world it is the supremest bliss of that Sacred Heart to suffer pain.

V

LOVE OF GOD AND LOVE OF MAN

V

LOVE OF GOD AND LOVE OF MAN

*Thou shalt love the Lord thy God with thy whole heart . . .
and thy neighbour as thyself.* — LUKE X. 27.

WE have already considered two charges brought
against Catholicism from opposite quarters; namely,
that we are too worldly and too otherworldly, too much
busied with temporal concerns to be truly spiritual, and
too metaphysical and remote and dogmatic to be truly
practical. Let us go on to consider these same two
charges produced, so to speak, a little further into a
more definitely spiritual plane; charges that now accuse
us of too great activities in our ministry to men and
too many attentions paid to God.

I. (i) It is a very common complaint against Catholics, laymen as well as clergy, that they are overzealous in
their attempts to proselytize. True and spiritual religion, we are told, is as intimate and personal an affair as
the love between husband and wife; it is essentially private and individual. "The religion of all sensible men,"
it has been said, "is precisely that which they always
keep to themselves." Tolerance, therefore, is a mark

of spirituality, for if I am truly religious I shall have as much respect for the religion of my neighbour as for my own. I shall no more seek to interfere in his relations with God than I shall allow him to interfere with mine.

Now Catholics are notoriously intolerant. It is not merely that there are intolerant Catholics, for intolerance is of course to be found in all narrow-minded persons, but it is Catholic principles themselves that are intolerant; and every Catholic who lives up to them is bound to be so also. And we can see this illustrated every day.

First, there is the matter of Catholic missions to the heathen. There are no missionaries, we are told, so untiring and so devoted as those of the Church. Their zeal, of course, is a proof of their sincerity; but it is also a proof of their intolerance: for why, after all, cannot they leave the heathen alone, since religion is, in its essence, a private and individual matter? Beautiful pictures, accordingly, are suggested to us of the domestic peace and happiness reigning amongst the tribes of Central Africa until the arrival of the Preaching Friar with his destructive dogmas. We are bidden to observe the high doctrines and the ascetic life of the Brahmin, the significant symbolism of the Hindu, and the philosophical attitudes of the Confucian. All these various relationships to God are, we are informed, entirely the private affairs of those who live by them; and if Catholics were truly spiritual they would understand that this was so and not seek to supplant by a system which is now, at any rate, become an essentially European way of looking at things, these ancient creeds and philosophies that are far better suited to the Oriental temperament.

But the matter is worse, even, than this. It may conceivably be argued, says the modern man of the world, that after all those Oriental religions have not developed such virtues and graces as has Christianity. It may perhaps be argued that in time the religion of the West, if missionaries will persevere, will raise the Hindu higher than his own obscenities have succeeded in doing, and that the civilization produced by Christianity is actually of a higher type, in spite of its evil by-products, than that of the head-hunters of Borneo and the bloody savages of Africa. But at any rate there is no excuse whatever for the intolerant Catholic proselytizer in English homes. For, roughly speaking, it is only the Catholic whom you cannot trust in your own home circle; sooner or later you will find him, if he at all lives up to his principles, insinuating the praises of his own faith and the weaknesses of your own; your sons and daughters he considers to be fair game; he thinks nothing of your domestic peace in comparison with the propagation of his own tenets. He is characterized, first and last, by that dogmatic and intolerant spirit that is the exact contrary of all that the modern world deems to be the spirit of true Christianity. True Christianity, then, as has been said, is essentially a private, personal, and individual matter between each soul and her God.

(ii) The second charge brought against Catholics is that they make religion far too personal, too private, and too intimate for it to be considered the religion of Jesus Christ. And this is illustrated by the supreme value which the Church places upon what is known as the Contemplative Life.

For if there is one element in Catholicism that the man-in-the-street especially selects for reprobation it is the life of the Enclosed Religious. It is supposed to be selfish, morbid, introspective, unreal; it is set in violent dramatic contrast with the ministerial Life of Jesus Christ. A quantity of familiar eloquence is solemnly poured out upon it as if nothing of the kind had ever been said before: it is said that "a man cannot get away from the world by shutting himself up in a monastery"; that "a man should not think about his own soul so much, but rather of what good he can do in the world in which God has placed him"; that "four whitewashed walls" are not the proper environment for a philanthropic Christian.

And yet, after all, what is the Contemplative Life except precisely that which the world just now recommended? And could religion possibly be made a more intimate, private, and personal matter between the soul and God than the Carthusian or Carmelite makes it?

The fact is, of course, that Catholics are wrong whatever they do — too extreme in everything which they undertake. They are too active and not retired enough in their proselytism; too retired and not active enough in their Contemplation.

II. Now the Life of our Divine Lord exhibits, of course, both the Active and the Contemplative elements that have always distinguished the Life of His Church.

For three years He set Himself to the work of preaching His Revelation and establishing the Church that was to be its organ through all the centuries. He went about, therefore, freely and swiftly, now in town, now in country. He laid down His Divine principles and presented His Divine credentials, at marriage feasts, in market-places, in country roads, in crowded streets, and in private houses. He wrought the works of mercy, spiritual and corporal, that were to be the types of all works of mercy ever afterwards. He gave spiritual and ascetic teaching on the Mount of Beatitudes, dogmatic instructions in Capharnaum and the wilderness to the east of Galilee, and mystical discourses in the Upper Chamber of Jerusalem and the temple courts. His activities and His proselytisms were unbounded. He broke up domestic circles and the routine of offices. He called the young man from his estates and Matthew from custom-house and James and John from their father's fishing business. He made a final demonstration of His unlimited claim on humanity in His Proces-

sion on Palm Sunday, and on Ascension Day ratified
and commissioned the proselytizing activities of His
Church for ever in His tremendous charge to the Apos-
tolic band. *Going, therefore, teach ye all nations . . .
teaching them to observe all things whatsoever I have commanded you; and behold I am with you all the days, even
to the consummation of the world.*

Yet this, it must be remembered, was not only not
the whole of His Life on earth, it was not even a very
considerable part of it, if reckoned by years. For three
years He was active, but for thirty He was retired in
the house of Nazareth; and even those three years are
again and again broken by retirement. He is now in
the wilderness for forty days, now on the mountain all
night in prayer, now bidding His disciples come apart
and rest themselves. The very climax of His ministry
too was wrought in silence and solitude. He removed
Himself *about a stone's throw* in the garden of Gethsemane
from those who loved Him best; He broke His silence
on the Cross to bid farewell even to His holy Mother
herself. Above all, he explicitly and emphatically commended the Life of Contemplative Prayer as the highest
that can be lived on earth, telling Martha that activity,
even in the most necessary duties, was not after all the
best use to which time and love could be put, but rather
that *Mary had chosen the best part . . . the one thing that
is necessary*, and that it *shall not be taken away from her*
even by a sister's loving zeal.

Finally, fault was found with Jesus Christ, as with His Church, on precisely these two points. When He was living the life of retirement in the country He was rebuked that He did not go up to the feast and state His claims plainly — justify, that is, by activity, His pretensions to the Messiahship; and when He did so, He was entreated to bid his acclaimants *to hold their peace* — to justify, that is, by humility and retirement, His pretensions to spirituality.

III. The reconciliation, therefore, of these two elements in the Catholic system is very easy to find.

(i) First, it is the Church's Divinity that accounts for her passion for God. To her as to none else on earth is the very face of God revealed as the Absolute and Final Beauty that lies beyond the limits of all Creation. She in her Divinity enjoys it may be said, even in her sojourn on earth, that very Beatific Vision that enraptured always the Sacred Humanity of Jesus Christ. With all the company of heaven then, with Mary Immaculate, with the Seraphim and with the glorified saints of God, she *endures, seeing Him Who is invisible.* Even while the eyes of her humanity are held, while her human members *walk by faith and not by sight,* she, in her Divinity, which is the guaranteed Presence of Jesus Christ in her midst, already *dwells in heavenly places* and is already *come to Mount Zion and the City of the living God and to God Himself,* Who is the Light in which all fair things are seen to be fair.

Is it any wonder then that, now and again, some chosen child of hers catches a mirrored glimpse of what she herself beholds with unveiled face; that some Catholic soul, now and again, chosen and called by God to this amazing privilege, should suddenly perceive, as never before, that God is the one and only Absolute Beauty, and that, compared with the contemplation of this Beauty — which contemplation is, after all, the final life of Eternity to which every redeemed soul shall come — all the activities of earthly life are nothing; and that, in her passion for this adorable God, she should run into a secret room and *shut the door and pray to her Father Who is in secret*, and so remain praying, a hidden channel of life to the whole of that Body of which she is a member, an intercessor for the whole of that Society of which she is one unit? There in silence, then, she sits at Jesus' feet and listens to the Voice which is *as the sound of many waters;* in the whiteness of her cell watches Him Whose *Face is as a Flame of Fire*, and in austerity and fasting *tastes and finds that the Lord is gracious.*

Of course this is but madness and folly to those who know God only in His Creation, who imagine Him merely as the Soul of the World and the Vitality of Created Life. To such as these earth is His highest Heaven and the beauty of the world the noblest vision that can be conceived. Yet to that soul that is Catholic, who understands that the Eternal Throne is indeed above the stars and that the Transcendence of God is as fully

a truth as His Immanence — that God in Himself, apart
from all that He has made, is all-fair and all-sufficient
in His own Beauty — to such a soul as this, if called to
such a life, there is no need that the Church should
declare explicitly that the Contemplative Life is the
highest. She knows it already.

(ii) The *First Great Commandment* of the Law, then,
is inevitably followed by the Second, and the Catholic
interpretation of the Second is thought by the world,
which understands neither, to be as extravagant as her
interpretation of the First.

For this Divine Church that knows God is also a
Human Society that dwells among men, and since she
in herself unites Divinity and Humanity, she cannot
rest until she has united them everywhere else.

For, as she turns her eyes from God to men, she sees
there immortal souls, made in the image of God and
made for Him and Him alone, seeking to satisfy themselves with Creation instead of with the Creator. She
hears how the world preaches the sanctity of the temperament, and the holiness of the individual point of
view, as if there were no Transcendent God at all and
no objective external Revelation ever made by Him.
She sees how men, instead of seeking to conform themselves to God's Revelation of Himself, attempt rather
to conform such fragments of that Revelation as have
reached them to their own points of view; she listens to
talk about "aspects of truth" and "schools of thought"

and the "values of experience" as if God had never spoken either in the thunders of Sinai or the still voice of Galilee.

Is it any wonder, then, that her Proselytism appears to such a world as extravagant as her Contemplation, her passion for men as unreasonable as her passion for God, when that world sees her bring herself from her cloisters and her secret places to proclaim as with a trumpet those demands of God which He has made known, those Laws which He has promulgated, and those rewards which He has promised? For how can she do otherwise who has looked on the all-glorious Face of God and then on the vacant and complacent faces of men — she who knows God's infinite capacity for satisfying men and men's all but infinite incapacity for seeking God — when she sees some poor soul shutting herself up indeed within the deadly and chilly walls of her own "temperament" and "individual point of view," when earth and heaven and the Lord of them both is waiting for her outside?

The Church, then, is too much interested in men and too much absorbed in God. Of course she is too much interested and too much absorbed, for she alone knows the value and capacity of both; she who is herself both Divine and Human. For Religion, to her, is not an elegant accomplishment or a graceful philosophy or a pleasing scheme of conjectures. It is the fiery bond between God and man, neither of whom can be satisfied without the other, the One in virtue of His Love and the other in virtue of his createdness. She alone, then, understands and reconciles the tremendous Paradox of the Law that is Old as well as New. *Thou shalt love the Lord thy God with thy whole heart . . . and thy neighbour as thyself.*

VI

FAITH AND REASON

VI

FAITH AND REASON

Whosoever shall not receive the kingdom of God as a little child shall not enter into it. — MARK X. 15.

Some things hard to be understood, which the unlearned and the unstable wrest, as also the other Scriptures, to their own perdition. — II PET. III. 16.

THERE are two great gifts, or faculties, by which men attain to truth: faith and reason. From these two sides, therefore, come two more assaults upon the Catholic position, a position which itself faces in both these directions. On the one side we are told that we believe too simply, on the other that we do not believe simply enough; on the one side that we reason too little, on the other that we do not reason enough. Let us set out these attacks in order.

I. (i) "You Catholics," says one critic, "are far too credulous in matters of religion. You believe, not as reasonable men believe, because you have verified or experienced the truths you profess, but simply because these dogmas are presented to you by the Church. If reason and common-sense are gifts of God and intended for use, surely it is very strange to silence them in your search for the supreme truth. Faith, of course, has its place, but it must not be blind faith. Reason must test, verify, and interpret, or faith is mere credulity.

"Consider, for example, the words of Christ, *This is My Body*. Now the words as they stand may certainly be supposed to mean what you say they mean; yet, interpreted by Reason, they cannot possibly mean anything of the kind. Did not Christ Himself sit in bodily form at the table as He spoke them? How then could He hold Himself in His hand? Did He not speak in metaphors and images continually? Did He not call Himself *a Door and a Vine?* Using Reason, then, to interpret these words, it is evident that He meant no more than that He was instituting a memorial feast, in which the bread should symbolize His Body and the wine His Blood. So too with many other distinctively Catholic doctrines—with the Petrine claims, with the authority 'to bind and loose,' and the rest. Catholic belief on these points exhibits not faith properly so-called — that is, Faith tested by Reason — but mere credulity. God gave us all Reason! Then in His Name let us use it!"

(ii) From the other side comes precisely the opposite charge.

"You Catholics," cries the other critic, "are far too argumentative and deductive and logical in your Faith. True Religion is a very simple thing; it is the attitude of a child who trusts and does not question. But with you Catholics Religion has degenerated into Theology. Jesus Christ did not write a *Summa;* He made a few plain statements which comprise, as they stand, the whole Christian Religion; they are full of mystery, no doubt, but it is He who left them mysterious. Why, then, should your theologians seek to penetrate into regions which He did not reveal and to elaborate what He left unelaborated?

"Take, for example, Christ's words, *This is My Body.* Now of course these words are mysterious, and if Christ had meant that they should be otherwise, He would Himself have given the necessary comment upon them. Yet He did not; He left them in an awful and deep simplicity into which no human logic ought even to seek to penetrate. Yet see the vast and complicated theology that the traditions have either piled upon them or attempted to extract out of them; the philosophical theories by which it has been sought to elucidate them; the intricate and wide-reaching devotions that have been founded upon them! What have words like 'Transubstantiation' and 'Concomitance,' devotions like 'Benediction,' gatherings like Eucharistic Congresses to do with the august simplicity of Christ's own institution? You Catholics argue too much — deduce, syllogize, and explain — until the simple splendour of Christ's mysterious act is altogether overlaid and hidden. Be more simple! It is better to '*love God than to discourse learnedly about the Blessed Trinity.' It has not pleased God to save His people through dialectics.* Believe more, argue less!"

Once more, then, the double charge is brought. We believe, it seems, where we ought to reason. We reason where we ought to believe. We believe too blindly and not blindly enough. We reason too closely and not closely enough.

Here, then, is a vast subject — the relations of Faith and Reason and the place of each in man's attitude towards Truth. It is, of course, possible only to glance at these things in outline.

II. First, let us consider, as a kind of illustration, the relations of these things in ordinary human science. Neither Faith nor Reason will, of course, be precisely the same as in supernatural matters; yet there will be a sufficient parallel for our purpose.

A scientist, let us say, proposes to make observations upon the structure of a fly's leg. He catches his fly, dissects, prepares, places it in his microscope, observes, and records. Now here, it would seem, is Pure Science at its purest and Reason in its most reasonable aspect. Yet the acts of faith in this very simple process are, if we consider closely, simply numberless. The scientist must make acts of faith, certainly reasonable acts, yet none the less of faith, for all that: first, that his fly is not a freak of nature; next, that his lens is symmetrically ground; then that his observation is adequate; then that his memory has not played him false between his observing and his recording that which he has seen. These acts are so reasonable that we forget that they are acts of faith. They are justified by reason before they are made, and they are usually, though not invariably, verified by Reason afterwards. Yet they are, in their essence, Faith and not Reason.

So, too, when a child learns a foreign language. Reason justifies him in making one act of faith that his teacher is competent, another that his grammar is correct, a third that he hears and sees and understands correctly the information given him, a fourth that such a language actually exists. And when he visits France afterwards he can, within limits, again verify by his reason the acts of faith which he has previously made. Yet none the less they were acts of faith, though they were reasonable.

In a word, then, no acquirement of or progress in any branch of human knowledge is possible without the exercise of faith. I cannot walk downstairs in the dark without at least as many acts of faith as there are steps in the staircase. Society could not hold together another day if mutual faith were wholly wanting among its units. Certainly we use reason first to justify our faith, and we reason later to verify it. Yet none the less the middle step is faith. Columbus reasoned first that there must be a land beyond the Atlantic, and he used that same reason later to verify his discovery. Yet without a sublime act of faith between these pro-

cesses, without that almost reckless moment in which
he first weighed anchor from Europe, reason would
never have gone beyond speculative theorizing. Faith
made real for him what Reason suggested. Faith
actually accomplished that of which Reason could only
dream.

III. Turn now to the coming of Jesus Christ on earth.
He came, as we know now, a Divine Teacher from
heaven to make a Revelation from God; He came, that
is, to demand from men a˥sublime Act of Faith in Himself. For He Himself was Incarnate Wisdom, and He
demanded, therefore, as none else can demand it, a
supreme acceptance of His claim. No progress in
Divine knowledge, as He Himself tells us, is possible,
then, without this initial act. *Whosoever shall not
receive the kingdom of God as a little child shall not
enter into it*. Every soul that is to receive this teaching
in its entirety must first accept the Teacher and sit
at His feet.

Yet He did not make this claim merely on His own
unsupported word. He presented His credentials, so to
say; He fulfilled prophecy; He wrought miracles; He
satisfied the moral sense. *Believe Me*, He says, *for the
very works' sake*. Before, then, demanding the fundamental act of Faith on which the reception of Revelation must depend, He took pains to make this Act of
Faith reasonable. "You see what I do," He said in
effect, "you have observed My life, My words, My

actions. Now is it not in accordance with Reason that you should grant My claims? Can you explain away, *reasonably*, on any other grounds than those which I state, the phenomena of My life?"

Certainly, then, He appealed to Reason; He appealed to Private Judgment, since that, up to that moment, was all that His hearers possessed. But, in demanding an Act of Faith, He appealed to Private Judgment to set itself aside; He appealed to Reason as to whether it were not Reasonable to stand aside for the moment and let Faith take its place. And we know how His disciples responded. *Whom do you say that I am? . . . Thou art the Christ, the Son of the Living God.*

At that instant, then, a new stage was begun. They had used their Reason and their Private Judgment, and, aided by His grace, had concluded that the next reasonable step was that of Faith. Up to that point they had observed, dissected, criticized, and analyzed His words; they had examined, that is, His credentials. And now it was Reason itself that urged them towards Faith, Reason that abdicated what had hitherto been, its right and its duty, that Faith might assume her proper place. Henceforth, then, their attitude must be a different one. Up to now they had used their Reason to examine His claim; now it was Faith, aided and urged by Reason, which accepted it.

Yet even now Reason's work is not done, though its scope in future is changed. Reason no longer examines

whether He be God; Faith has accepted it: yet Reason
has to be as active as ever; for Reason now must begin
with all its might the task of understanding His Revelation. Faith has given them, so to speak, casket after
casket of jewels; every word that Jesus Christ henceforth speaks to them is a very mine of treasure, absolutely true since He is known to be a Divine Teacher
Who has given it. And Reason now begins her new
work, not of justifying Faith, but, so to say, of inter-
preting it; not of examining His claims, since these
have been once for all accepted, but of examining,
understanding, and assimilating all that He reveals.

III. Turn now to Catholicism.

It is the Catholic Church, and the Catholic Church
only, that acts as did Jesus Christ and offers an adequate
object to Reason and Faith alike. For, first, it is evident that if Christ intended His Revelation to last
through all time, He must have designed a means by
which it should last, an Authority that should declare
and preserve it as He Himself delivered it. And next,
it is evident that since the Catholic Church alone even
claims that prerogative, clearly and coherently, her
right to represent that Authority is in proportion to the
clearness and coherence of her claim. Or, again, she
advances in support of that claim precisely those same
credentials as did He: she points to her miracles, her
achievements, the fulfilment of prophecy, the unity of her
teaching, the appeal to men's moral sense — all of them

appeals to Reason, and appeals which lead up, as did His, to the supreme claim, which He also made, to demand an Act of Faith in herself as a Divine Teacher.

For she alone demands it. Other denominations of Christendom point to a Book, or to the writings of Fathers, or to the example of their members, and she too does these things. But it is she alone who appeals to these things not as final in themselves, not as constituting in themselves a final court of appeal, but as indicating as that court of appeal her own Living Voice. *Believe me, for the works' sake*, she too says. "Use your reason to the full to examine my credentials; study prophecy, history, the Fathers — study my claims in any realm in which your intellect is competent — and then see if it is not after all supremely reasonable for Reason to abdicate that particular throne on which she has sat so long and to seat Faith there instead? Certainly follow your Reason and use your private judgment, for at present you have no other guide; and then, please God, aided by Faith, Reason will itself bow before Faith, and take her own place henceforth, not on the throne, but on the steps that lead to it."

Is Reason, then, to be silent henceforth? Why, the whole of theology gives the answer. Did Newman cease to think when he became a Catholic? Did Thomas Aquinas resign his intellect when he devoted himself to study? Not for one instant is Reason silent. On the contrary, she is active as never before. Certainly she is no longer occupied in examining as to whether the Church is divine, but instead she is busied, with incredible labours, in examining what follows from that fact, in sorting the new treasures that are opened to her with the dawn of Revelation upon her eyes, in arranging, deducting, and understanding the details and structure of the astonishing Vision of Truth. And more, she is as inviolate as ever. For never can there be presented to her one article of Faith that gives the lie to her own nature, since Revelation and Reason cannot contradict one the other. She has learned, indeed, that the mysteries of God often transcend her powers, that she cannot fathom the infinite with the finite; yet never for one moment is she bidden to evacuate her own position or believe that which she perceives to be untrue. She has learned her limitations, and with that has come to understand her inviolable rights.

See, then, how the features of Christ look out through the lineaments of His Church. She alone dares to claim an act of Divine Faith in herself, since it is He Who speaks in her Voice. She alone, since she is Divine, bids the wisest men *become as little children* at her feet and endows little children with the wisdom of the ancients. Yet, on the other hand, in her magnificent Humanity, she has produced through the exercise of illuminated human Reason such a wealth of theology as the world has never seen. Is it any wonder that the world thinks both her Faith and Reason alike too ex-

treme? For her Faith rises from her Divinity and her
Reason from her Humanity; and such an outpouring of
Divinity and such an emphatic Humanity, such a superb
confidence in God's revelation and such untiring labours
upon the contents of that Revelation, are altogether
beyond the imagination of a world that in reality, fears
both Faith and Reason alike.

At her feet, and hers only, then, do the wisest and the
simple kneel together — St. Thomas and the child, St.
Augustine and the "charcoal burner"; as diverse, in
their humanity, as men can be; as united in the light of
Divinity as only those can be who have found it.

So, then, she goes forward to victory. "First use
your reason," she cries to the world, "to see whether I
be not Divine! Then, impelled by Reason and aided
by Grace, rise to Faith. Then once more call up your
Reason, to verify and understand those mysteries which
you accept as true. And so, little by little, vistas of
truth will open about you and doctrines glow with an
undreamed-of light. So Faith will be interpreted by
Reason and Reason hold up the hands of Faith, until
you come indeed to the unveiled vision of the Truth
whose feet already you grasp in love and adoration;
until you see, face to face in Heaven, Him Who is at
once the Giver of Reason and the *Author of Faith*." ˎ

VII

AUTHORITY AND LIBERTY

AUTHORITY AND LIBERTY

The truth shall make you free. — JOHN VIII. 32.
Bringing into captivity every understanding to the obedience of Christ. — II COR. X. 5.

WE have already considered in outline the relations between Faith and Reason; how each, in its own province, is supreme and how each, in its turn, supports and ratifies the other. We pass on to a development of that theme, springing almost immediately out of it, namely, the relations between Authority and Liberty. And we will begin that consideration, as before, as it is illustrated by the accusations of the world against the Church. Briefly they are stated as follows.

I. Freedom, we are told, is the note of Christianity as laid down in the Gospels, in both discipline and doctrine. Jesus Christ came into the world largely for this very purpose, to substitute the New Law for the Old and thereby to free men from the complicated theology and the minutiæ of religious routine which characterized men's attempts to reduce that Old Law to practice. The Old Law may or may not have been perfectly adapted, when first it was given, to the needs of God's people in the early stages of Jewish civilization; but at any rate it is certain, from a hundred texts in the Gospel, that Jesus Christ in His day found it an intolerable slavery laid upon the religious life of the people. Theology had degenerated into an incredible hair-splitting system of dogma, and discipline had degenerated into a multitude of irritating observances.

Jesus Christ, then, in the place of all this, preached a Creed that was essentially simple, and simultaneously substituted for the elaborate ceremonialism of the Pharisees the spirit of liberty. The dogma that He preached was little more than that God is the Father of all and that all men therefore are brothers; "discipline" in the ordinary sense of the word is practically absent from the Gospel, and as for ceremonial there is none, except such as is necessary for the performance of the two extremely simple rites that He instituted, Baptism and the Lord's Supper.

Now this supposed spirit of liberty, we are informed, is to-day to be found only in Protestantism. In that system, if it can strictly be called one, and in that system only, may a man exercise that freedom which was secured to him by Jesus Christ. First, in doctrine, he may choose, weigh, and examine for himself, within the wide limits which alone Christ laid down, those doctrines or hopes which commend themselves to his intellect; and next, in matters of discipline, again, he may choose for himself those ways of life and action that he may find helpful to his spiritual development. He may worship, for example, in any church that he prefers, attend those services and those only which commend themselves to his taste; he may eat or not eat this or that food, as he likes, and order his day, generally, as it pleases him. And all this, we are informed, is of the very spirit of New Testament Christianity. *The Truth has made him free*, as Christ Himself promised.

The Catholic Church, on the other hand, is essentially a Church of slavery. First, in discipline, an enormous weight of observances and duties is laid upon her children, comparable only to the Pharisaic system. The Catholic must worship in this church and not in that, in this manner and not in the other. He must observe places and days and times, and that not only in religious matters but in secular. He must eat this food on this day and that on the other; he must frequent the sacraments at specified periods; he must perform certain actions and refrain from others, and that in matters in themselves indifferent.

In dogma, too, no less is the burden that he must bear. Not only are the simple words of Christ developed into a vast theological system by the Church's officials, but the whole of this system is laid, as of faith, down to its minutest details, on the shoulders of the unhappy believer. He may not choose between this or that theory of the mode of Christ's Presence in the Eucharist;

he must accept precisely that, and no other, which his Church has elaborated.

In fact, in doctrine and in discipline alike, the Church has gone back to precisely that old reign of tyranny which Christ abolished. The Catholic, unlike the Protestant who has retained the spirit of liberty, finds himself in the same case as that under which Israel itself once groaned. He is a slave and not a child; he binds his own limbs, as the old phrase says, by his act of faith and puts the other end of the chain into the hands of the priest. Such, in outline, is the charge against us.

Now much of it is so false that it needs no refutation. It is, for example, entirely false that New Testament theology is simple. It is far more true to say that, compared with the systematized theology of the Church, it is bewilderingly complex and puzzling, and how complex and puzzling it is, is indicated by the hundreds of creeds which Protestants have made out of it, each creed claiming, respectively, to be its one and only proper interpretation. Men have only come to think it "simple" in modern days by desperately eliminating from it every element on which all Protestants are not agreed. The residuum is indeed "simple." Only it is not the New Testament theology! Dogmas such as that of the Blessed Trinity, of the Procession of the Holy Ghost, of the nature of grace and of sin — these, whether as held by orthodox or unorthodox, are at any rate not simple, and it is merely untrue to say that Christ made no statements on these points, however they may be understood. Further, it is merely untrue to say that Protestant theology is "simple"; it is every whit as elaborate as Catholic theology and considerably more complex in those points in which Protestant divines are not agreed. The controversies on Justification in which such men as Calvin and Luther, with their disciples, continually engaged are fully as complicated as any disputations on Grace between Jesuits and Dominicans.

Yet the general contention is plain enough — that on the whole the Catholic is bound to believe a certain set of dogmas, while the Protestant is free to accept or reject them. Therefore, it is argued, the Protestant is "free" and the Catholic is not. And this brings us straight to the consideration of the relations between Authority and Liberty.

II. What, then, is Religious Liberty? It is necessary to begin by forming some idea as to what it is that is meant by the word in other than religious matters.

Very briefly it may be said that an individual enjoys social liberty when he is able to obey and to use the laws and powers of his true nature, and that a community enjoys it when all its members are able to do so without interfering unduly one with the other. The more complete is this ability, the more perfect is Liberty.

A remarkable paradox at once presents itself — that Liberty can only be secured by Laws. Where there are no laws, or too few, to secure it, slavery immediately appears, no less surely than when there are too many; for the stronger individuals are, by the absence of law, enabled to tyrannize over the weaker. Even the vast and complex legislation of our own days is designed to increase and not to fetter liberty, and its greater complexity is necessitated by the greater complexity and the more numerous interrelationships of modern society. Laws, of course, may be unwise or excessively minute or deliberately enslaving; yet this does not affect the point that for all that Laws are necessary to the preservation of Liberty. Merchants, women and children, and citizens generally, can only enjoy rightful liberty if they are protected by laws. Only that man is free, then, who is most carefully guarded.

In the same manner Scientific Liberty does not consist in the absence of knowledge, or of scientific dogmas, but in their presence. We are surrounded by innumerable facts of nature, and that man is free who is fully aware of those which affect his own life. It is true, for example, that two and two make four, and that heavy bodies tend to fall towards the centre of the earth; and it can only be a very superficial thinker who considers that to be ignorant of these facts is to be free from the enslaving dogmas of them. If I am ignorant of them I am, of course, in a sense at liberty to believe that two and two make five, and to jump off the roof of my house; yet this is not Liberty at all in the sense in which reasonable people use the word, since my knowledge of the laws enables me to be effective and, in fact, to survive in the midst of a world where they happen to be true. That man, then, is more truly "free" whose intellect is informed of and submits to these laws, than is the man whose intellect is unaware of them. Marconi's intellect submits to the laws of lightning and he is thereby enabled to avail himself of them. Ajax is unaware of them and is accordingly destroyed by their action.

The Truth, then, *makes us free*. The State which controls men's actions and educates their intellects, which, in a word, enforces the knowledge of truth and compels obedience to it, is actually freeing its citizens by that process. It is only by a misuse of words or a failure to grasp ideas that I can maintain that an ignorant savage is more free than an educated man. It is true that I am, in a sense, "free" to think that two and two make five, if I have not learned arithmetic; on the other hand, when I learn that they make four I rise into that higher and more real liberty which a knowledge of arithmetic bestows. I am more effective, not less so; I am more free to exercise my powers and use the forces of the world in which I live, and not less free, when I have submitted my intellect to facts.

III. (i) Now the soul too has an environment. Men may differ as to its nature and its conditions, but all who believe in the soul at all believe also that it has an environment, and that this environment is as much in the realm of Law as is the natural world itself. Prayer, for example, elevates the soul, base thinking degrades it.

Now the laws of this environment were true even before Christ came. David knew, at any rate, something of penitence and of the guilt of sin, and Nathan knew something, at least, of the forgiveness of sins and of their temporal punishment. Christ came, then, with this object amongst others: that He might reveal the laws of Grace and convey to men's minds some at least of the facts of the spiritual life amongst which they lived. He came, moreover, partly to modify the workings of these laws, to release some more fully, and to restrain others; in a word, to be the Revealer of Truth and the Administrator of Grace.

He came then, to increase men's liberty by increasing their knowledge, as, in another sphere, the scientist comes to us with the same purpose. Here, for example, is the law that murder is a sin before God and brings its consequences with it, a law stated briefly in the commandment *Thou shalt not kill*. But our Divine Lord revealed more of the workings of this law than men had hitherto recognized. *I say unto you*, declared Christ, *that whosoever hateth his brother is a murderer*. He revealed, that is to say, the fact that this law runs even in the realm of thought, that the hating spirit incurs the guilt and punishment of murder, and not merely the murderous action. Were men less free when they learned that fact? Not unless I am less free than I was before, when I learn for the first time that lightning kills. Christ came, then, to reveal the *Truth that makes us free,* and He does so by informing our intellects and enabling us to *bring into captivity every understanding to His obedience.*

(ii) Turn now to the Catholic Church. Here is a Society whose function it is to preserve and apply the teaching of Christ; to analyze it and to state it in forms or systems which every generation can receive. For this purpose, then, she draws up not merely a Creed— which is the systematic statement of the Christian Revelation—but disciplinary rules and regulations that will make this Creed and the life that is conformable to it more easy of realization, and all this she does with the express object of enabling the individual soul to respond to her spiritual environment and to rise to the full exercise of her powers and rights. As the scientist and the statesmen take, respectively, the great laws of nature and society and reduce them to rules and codes, yet without adding or taking away from these facts, that are true whether they are popularly recognized or not — and all with the purpose not of diminishing but of increasing the general liberty — so the Church, divinely safeguarded too in the process, takes the Revelation of Christ and by her dogma and her discipline popularizes it, so to speak, and makes it at once comprehensible and effective.

What, then, is this foolish cry about the slavery of

dogma? How can Truth make men anything except more free? Unless a man is prepared to say that the scientist enslaves his intellect by telling him facts, he dare not say that the Church fetters his intellect by defining dogma. Christ did not condemn the Pharisaic system because it was a system, but because it was Pharisaic; because, that is, it was not true; because it obscured instead of revealing the true relations between God and man; because it *made the Word of God of none effect through its traditions.*

But the Catholic system has the appearance of enslaving men? Why yes; for the only way of aiming at and using effectively the *truth that makes us free* is by *bringing into captivity every understanding to the obedience of Christ.*

VIII
CORPORATENESS AND INDIVIDUALISM

VIII

CORPORATENESS AND INDIVID-
UALISM

*He that shall lose his life for My sake shall find it. For
what doth it profit a man if he gain the whole world and
suffer the loss of his own soul?* — MATT. XVI. 25, 26.

No recorded word of our Lord better illustrates than
does this the startling and paradoxical manner of His
teaching. For He Who *knew what was in man*, Who
spoke always down to man's deepest interests, dwelt
and spoke therefore in that realm of truth where man's
own paradoxical nature is most manifest; where his
interests appear to flourish only by being ruthlessly
pruned; where he rises to the highest development of
self only by self-mortification. This is, in fact, the very
lesson Christ teaches in these words. To *find the life* is
the highest object of every man and the end for which
he was created; yet this can be attained only by the
losing of it for Christ's sake. Individuality can be preserved only by the sacrifice of Individualism. Let us
break up this thought and consider it more in detail.

I. (i) Catholics, it is said, are the most fundamentally
selfish people in the whole world, since all that they do

and say and think is directed and calculated, so far as
they are "good Catholics," to the salvation of their own
souls. It is this that continually crops up in their con-
versation, and this that presumably is their chief pre-
occupation. Yet surely this, above all methods, is
the very worst for achieving such an end. One does
not pull up flowers to see how they are growing. The
very secret of health is to be unconscious of it. Catholics, on the other hand, scarcely ever do anything else;
they are for ever examining themselves, for ever going
to confession, for ever developing and cultivating the
narrowest virtues. The whole science of Casuistry, for
example, is directed to nothing else but this — the exact
definition of those limits within which the salvation of
the soul is secure and beyond which it is imperilled; and
Casuistry, as we all know, has a stifling and deadening
influence upon all who study it.

Again, see how the true development and expansion
of the soul must necessarily be hindered by such an
ideal. "I must not read this book, however brilliant,
since it might be dangerous to my faith. I must not
mix in this company, however charming, since evil com-
munications corrupt good manners." What kind of
life is that which must always be checked and stunted
in this fashion? What kind of salvation can there be
that can only be purchased by the sacrifice of so much
that is noble and inspiring? True life consists in experience, not in introspection; in going out from self into

the world, not in retiring from the world inwards. Let
us therefore live our life without fear, lose ourselves in
humanity, forget self in experience, and leave the rest
to God!

(ii) So much for the one side, while from the other
comes almost precisely the opposite criticism. Catholics, it is said, are not nearly individualistic enough; on
the contrary they are for ever sinking themselves and
their personalities in the corporate life of the Church.
Not only are their outward actions checked and their
words guarded, but even their very consciences and
thoughts are informed and made by the collective conscience and mind of others. It is the highest ambition
of every good Catholic *sentire cum ecclesia;* not merely
to act and speak but even to think in obedience to others.
Now a man's true life, we are told, consists in an assertion
of his own individuality. God has made no two men the
same; the mould was made and broken in each several
case. If, therefore, we are to be what He meant us to be,
we must make the most of our own personalities; we
must think our own thoughts, not other people's, direct
our own lives, speak our own minds — so far, of course,
as we can do so without interfering with our neighbour's
equal liberty. Once more, therefore, we are bidden to
live our life to the full; not in this case, however, because
we all share in a common humanity, but because we do
not!

We Catholics are wrong, therefore, for both reasons

and in both directions. We are wrong when we put self first and we are wrong when we do not. We are wrong when we launch out into the current of life, and wrong when we withdraw ourselves from its waters. We are wrong when we insist upon our personal responsibility, and wrong when we look to the Church to undertake it.

II. (i) Here then, indeed, is a Paradox; but it is one which our Lord Himself expressly emphasizes. For, first, there is nothing on which He so repeatedly insists as the supreme and singular value of every soul's salvation. If this is not attained, all is lost. *What shall it profit a man if he shall gain the whole world and suffer the loss of his own soul?* All else, then, must be sacrificed if this is in peril. No human possession, however great, can be weighed against this. No human tie, however sacred, can hold against its claim. Not only must *houses and lands,* but *father and mother and wives and children* must take second place, so soon as eternal life is at stake. And yet, somehow or another, this salvation can only be attained by loss; self can only live if it be mortified, can only be saved by its own denial. Individuality, as has been said, can only be preserved by the loss of Individualism.

(ii) But this is not peculiar to the spiritual sphere; it is a paradox that is true, in some sense, of life on every plane — civic, intellectual, artistic, human. The man that desires to bring his intellectual and personal powers

to their highest pitch must continually be sinking
them, so to speak, in the current of his fellows, continually exhausting, using, and wearing them out. He must
risk, and indeed inevitably lose, in a very real sense, his
personal point of view, if he is to have a point of view
that is worth possessing; he must be content to see his
theories and his thoughts modified, merged, changed,
and destroyed, if his thought is to be of value. For, so
far as he withdraws himself from his fellows into a
physical or mental isolation, so far he approaches ego-
tistic madness. He cannot grow unless he decreases; he
cannot remain himself unless he ceases to be himself.

So, too, is it in civic and artistic life. The citizen
who truly lives to the State of which he is a member
— the man to whom his country raises a monument, for
example — is one, always, who has *lost himself* for his
nation, whether he has died in battle or sacrificed himself in politics or philanthropy. And the citizen who
has merely hugged his citizenship to himself, who has
enjoyed all the privileges he can get and paid nothing
for them, — least of all himself — who has, so to say,
gained the whole world, has simultaneously lost himself
indeed and is forgotten within a year of his death. So
with the artist. The man who has made his art serve
him, who has employed it, let us say, purely for the
sake of the money he could get out of it, who has kept
it within severe limits, who has been merely prudent
and orderly and restrained, this man has, in a sense,

saved his own life; yet simultaneously he has lost it.
But the man to whom art is a passion, to whom nothing
else is comparatively of any value, who has plunged
himself in his art, has dedicated to it his days and his
nights, has sacrificed to it every power of his being
and every energy of his mind and body, this man has
indeed *lost himself.* Yet he lives in his art as the other
has not, he has *saved himself* in a sense of which the
other knows nothing; and exactly in proportion as
he has succeeded in his self-abnegation, so far has he
attained, as we say, immortality. There is not, then,
one sphere of life in which the paradox is not true.
The great historical lovers in romance, the pioneers
of science, the immortals in every plane, are precisely
those that have fulfilled on lower levels the spiritual
aphorism of Jesus Christ.

(iii) Turn, then, once more to the Catholic Church and
see how in the Life which she offers, as in none other,
there is presented to us a means of fulfilling our end.

For it is she alone who even demands in the spiritual
sphere a complete and entire abnegation of self. From
every other Christian body comes the cry, Save your
soul, assert your individuality, follow your conscience,
form your opinions; while she, and she alone, demands
from her children the sacrifice of their intellect, the
submitting of their judgment, the informing of their
conscience by hers, and the obedience of their will to
her lightest command. For she, and she alone, is con-

scious of possessing that Divinity, in complete sub-
mission to which lies the salvation of Humanity.   For
she, as the coherent and organic mystical Body of
Christ, calls upon those who look to her to become,
not merely her children, but her very members; not to
obey her as soldiers obey a leader or citizens a Government, but as the hands and eyes and feet obey a brain.
Once, therefore, I understand this, I understand too
how it is that by being lost in her I save myself;
that I lose only that which hinders my activity, not
that which fosters it.   For when is my hand most itself?
When separated from the body, by paralysis or amputa-
tion?   Or when, in vital union with the brain, with
every fibre alert and every nerve alive, it obeys in every
gesture and receives in every sensation a life infinitely
vaster and higher than any which it might, temporarily,
enjoy in independence?   It is true that its capacity for
pain is the greater when it is so united, and that it
would cease to suffer if once its separation were accomplished; yet, simultaneously, it would lose all that for
which God made it and, *saving itself*, would be *lost*
indeed.

I live, then, the perfect Catholic may say, as none
other can say, when I have ceased to be myself.   And
yet not I, since I have lost my Individualism.   No longer
do I claim any activity at all on my own behalf; no
longer do I demand to form my opinions, to follow my
own conscience apart from that informing of it that

comes from God, or to live my own life. Yet in losing my Individualism I have won my Individuality, for I have found my true place at last. I have *lost the whole world?* Yes, so far as that world is separate from or antagonistic to God's will; but I have *gained my own soul* and attained immortality. For it is *not I that live, but Christ that liveth in me.*

IX

MEEKNESS AND VIOLENCE

MEEKNESS AND VIOLENCE

Blessed are the meek. — MATT. V. 4.
The Kingdom of Heaven suffereth violence, and the violent
bear it away. — MATT. XI. 12.

WE have already considered the Church's relations
towards such things as wealth and human influence and
power, how she will sometimes use and sometimes dis-
dain them. Let us now penetrate a little deeper and
understand the spirit that underlies and explains this
varying attitude of hers.

I. (i) It has been charged against Christianity in
general, and therefore implicitly and supremely against
the Church that was for so long its sole embodiment
and is still, alone, its adequate representative, that it
has fostered virtues which retard progress. Progress,
in the view of the German philosopher who explicitly
made this charge, is merely natural both in its action
and its end; and Nature, as we are well aware, knows
nothing of forgiveness or compassion or tenderness: on
the contrary she moves from lower to higher forms by
forces that are their precise opposite. The wounded
stag is not protected by his fellows, but gored to death;

the old wolf is torn to pieces, the sick lion wanders away to die of starvation, and all these instincts, we are informed, have for their object the gradual improvement of the breed by the elimination of the weak and ineffective. So should it be, he tells us, with man, and the extreme Eugenists echo his teaching. Christianity, on the other hand, deliberately protects the weak and teaches that the sacrifice of the strong is supreme heroism. Christianity has raised hospitals and refuges for the infirm, seeking to preserve those very types which Nature, if she had her way, would eliminate. Christianity, then, is the enemy of the human race and not its friend, since Christianity has retarded, as no other religion has ever succeeded in retarding, the appearance of that superman whom Nature seeks to evolve. . . . It is scarcely to be wondered at that the teacher of such a doctrine himself died insane.

A parallel doctrine is taught largely to-day by persons who call themselves practical and businesslike. Meekness and gentleness and compassion, they tell their sons, are very elegant and graceful virtues for those who can afford them, for women and children who are more or less sheltered from the struggle of life, and for feeble and ineffective people who are capable of nothing else. But for men who have to make their own way in the world and intend to win success there, a more stern code is necessary; from these there is demanded such a rule of action as Nature herself dictates. Be self-confident and self-assertive then, not meek.   Remember that the weakness of your neighbour is your own opportunity. Take care of number one and let the rest take care of themselves.   A man does not go into the stock-exchange or into commerce in order to exhibit Christian virtues there, but business qualities.   In a word, Christianity, so far as it affects material or commercial or political progress, is a weakness rather than a strength, an enemy rather than a friend.

(ii) But if, on the one side, the gentleness and non-resistance inculcated by Christianity form the material of one charge against the Church, on the other side, no less, she is blamed for her violence and intransigeance. Catholics are not yielding enough, we are told, to be true followers of the meek Prophet of Galilee, not gentle enough to inherit the blessing which He pronounced. On the contrary there are no people so tenacious, so obstinate, and even so violent as these professed disciples of Jesus Christ.   See the way, for example, in which they cling to and insist upon their rights; the obstacles they raise, for example, to reasonable national schemes of education or to a sensible system in the divorce courts.   And above all, consider their appalling and brutal violence as exhibited in such institutions as that of the Index and Excommunication, the fierceness with which they insist upon absolute and detailed obedience to authority, the ruthlessness with which they cast out from their company those who will not pronounce their shibboleths. It is true that in these days they can only enforce their claims by spiritual threatenings and penalties, but history shows us that they would do more if they could. The story of the racks and the fires of the Inquisition shows plainly enough that the Church once used, and therefore, presumably, would use again if she could, carnal weapons in her spiritual warfare. Can anything be more unlike the gentle Spirit of Him Who, *when He was reviled, reviled not again;* of Him Who bade men to *learn of Him, for He was meek and lowly of heart,* and so *find rest to their souls?*

Here, then, is the Paradox, and here are two characteristics of the Catholic Church: that she is at once too meek and too self-assertive, too gentle and too violent. It is a paradox exactly echoed by our Divine Lord Himself, Who in the Upper Chamber bade His disciples who *had no sword* to *sell their cloaks and buy them,* and Who yet, in the garden of Gethsemane, commanded the one disciple who had taken Him at His word to *put up the sword into its sheath,* telling him that *they who took the sword should perish by it.* It is echoed yet again in His action, first in taking the scourge into His own Hand, in the temple courts, and then in baring His shoulders to that same scourge in the hands of others. How, then, is this Paradox to be reconciled?

II. The Church, let us remind ourselves again, is both Human and Divine.

(i) She consists of human persons, and those persons

are attached both to one another and to the world outside by a perfectly balanced system of human rights
known as the Law of Justice. This Law of Justice,
though coming indeed from God, is, in a sense, natural
and human; it exists to some extent in all societies, as
well as being closely defined and worked out in the Old
Law given on Sinai. It is a Law which men could have
worked out, at any rate in its main principles, by the
light of reason only, unaided by Revelation, and it is a
Law, further, so fundamental that no Revelation could
conceivably ever outrage or set it aside.

At the coming of Christ into the world, however,
Supernatural Charity came with Him. The Law of
Justice still remained; men still had their rights on
which they might insist, still had their rights which no
Christian may refuse to recognize. But such was the
torrent of Divine generosity which Christ exhibited, so
overwhelming was the Vision which He revealed of the
supernatural charity of God towards men, that a set
of ideals sprang into life such as the world had never
dreamed of; more, Charity came with such power that
her commands actually overruled in many instances the
feeble claims of Justice, so that she bade men henceforward to forgive, for example, not merely according
to Justice, but according to her own Divine nature, to
forgive unto seventy times seven, to give *good measure,
heaped up and running over*, and not the bare minimum
which men had merely earned.

It was from this advent of Charity, then, that all these essentially Christian virtues of generosity and meekness and self-sacrifice sprang which Nietsche condemned as hostile to material progress.

For, from henceforth, *if a man take thy coat, let him take thy cloak also; if he will compel thee to go with him one mile, go two; if he strike thee on one cheek, turn to him the other also.* The Law of Natural Justice is transcended and the Law of Charity and Sacrifice reigns instead. *Resist not evil;* do not insist always, that is to say, on your natural rights; give men more than their due, and be yourself content with less. *Learn of Me, for I am meek and lowly of heart, and find rest to your souls. Forgive one another your trespasses* with the same generous charity with which God has forgiven and will forgive you yours. *Judge not and you shall not be judged.* Do not, in personal matters, insist upon bare justice for yourself, but act on that scale and by those principles by which God Himself has dealt with you.

Meekness, then, is undoubtedly a Christian virtue. Sometimes it is obligatory, sometimes it is but a Counsel of Perfection; it stands, in any case, high among those ideals which it has been the glory of Christianity to create.

(ii) But there are other elements in life besides the human and the natural, beyond those personal rights and claims which a Christian may, if he is aiming at

perfection, set aside out of charity.   The Church is
Divine as well as Human.

For the Church has entrusted to her, besides the rights
of men, which may be sacrificed by their possessors,
the rights and claims of God, which none but He can set
aside.   He has given into her keeping, for example, a
Revelation of truths and principles which, springing out
of His own Nature or of His Will, are as immutable and
eternal as Himself.   And it is precisely in defence of
these truths and principles that the Church exhibits that
which the world calls *intransigeance* and Jesus Christ
violence.

Here, for example, is the right of a baptized Catholic
child to be educated in his religion, or rather, the right
of God Himself to teach that child in the manner He
has ordained.   Here is the revealed truth that marriage
is indissoluble; here that Jesus Christ is the Son of God.
Now these are not human rights or opinions at all
—rights and opinions which men, urged by charity or
humility, can set aside or waive in the face of opposition.   They rest on an entirely different basis; they are,
so to speak, the inalienable possessions of God; and it
would neither be charity nor humility, but sheer treachery, for the Church to exhibit meekness or pliancy in
matters such as these, given to her as they are, not to
dispose of, but to guard intact.   On the contrary here,
exactly, comes the command, *He that hath not, let him
sell his cloak and buy a sword*, for here comes the line

between the Divine and the Human; let all personal possessions go, all merely natural rights and claims be yielded, and let a sword take their place. For here is a matter that must be *resisted, even unto blood.*

The Catholic Church then is, and always will be, *violent* and intransigeant when the rights of God are in question. She will be absolutely ruthless, for example, towards heresy, for heresy affects not personal matters on which Charity may yield, but a Divine right on which there must be no yielding. Yet, simultaneously, she will be infinitely kind towards the heretic, since a thousand human motives and circumstances may come in and modify his responsibility. At a word of repentance she will readmit his person into her treasury of souls, but not his heresy into her treasury of wisdom; she will strike his name eagerly and freely from her black list of the rebellious, but not his book from the pages of her Index. She exhibits meekness towards him and *violence* towards his error; since he is human, but her Truth is Divine.

It is, then, from a modern confusion of thought with regard to the realms of the Divine and the Human that the amazing inability arises, on the world's part, to understand the respective principles on which the Catholic Church acts in these two and utterly separate departments. The world considers it reasonable for a country to defend its material possessions by the sword, but intolerant and unreasonable for the Church to condemn, *resisting even unto blood,* principles which she considers erroneous or false. The Church, on the other hand, urges her children again and again to yield rather than to fight when merely material possessions are at stake, since Charity permits and sometimes even commands men to be content with less than their own rights, and yet again, when a Divine truth or right is at stake, here she will resist unfaltering and undismayed, since she cannot be "charitable" with what is not her own; here she will *sell her cloak* and *buy that sword* which, when the dispute was on merely temporal matters, she thrust back again into its sheath.

To-day [1] as Christ rides into Jerusalem we see, as in a mirror, this Paradox made plain. *Thy King cometh to thee, meek.* Was there ever so mean a Procession as this? Was there ever such meekness and charity? He Who, as His personal right, is attended in heaven by *a multitude on white horses,* now, in virtue of His Humanity, is content with a few fishermen and a crowd of children. He to Whom, in His personal right, the harpers and the angels make eternal music is content, since He has been made Man for our sakes, with the discordant shoutings of this crowd. He Who *rode on the Seraphim and came flying on the wings of the wind* sits on the colt of an ass. He comes, meek indeed, from the golden streets of the Heavenly Jerusalem to the foul roads of the Earthly, laying aside His personal rights

[1] This sermon was preached on Palm-Sunday.

since He is that very Fire of Charity by which Christians relinquish theirs.

But, for all that, it is *riding* that *thy King cometh to thee*. . . . He will not relinquish His inalienable claim and He will have nothing essential left out.   He has His royal escort, even though a ragged one; He will have His spearmen, even though their spears be only of palm; He will have His heralds to proclaim Him, however much the devout Pharisees may be offended by their proclamation; He will ride into His own Royal City, even though that City casts Him out, and He will have His Coronation, even though it be with thorns. So, too, the Catholic Church advances through the ages.

In merely human rights and personal matters again and again she will yield up all that she has, making, it may be, but one protest for Justice' sake and then no more.   And she will urge her children to do the same. If the world will let her have no jewels, then she will put glass beads in her monstrance, and for marble she will use plaster, and tinsel for gold.

But she will have her Procession and insist upon her Royalty.   It may seem as poor and as mean and as tawdry as the entrance of Christ Himself through the royal gate; for she will yield up all that the world demands of her, so long as her Divine Right itself remains intact.   She will issue her orders, though few be found to obey them; she will cast out from her the rebellious who question her authority, and cleanse her

Temple Courts even though with a scourge at which men mock. She will give up all that is merely human, if the world will have it so, and will *resist not evil* if it merely concerns herself. But there is one thing which she will not renounce, one thing she will claim, even with *violence* and "intransigeance," and that is the Royalty with which God Himself has crowned her.

X

THE SEVEN WORDS

X

THE SEVEN WORDS

THE "THREE HOURS"

INTRODUCTION

THE value, to the worshippers, of the Devotion of the Three Hours' Agony is in proportion to the degree in which they understand that they are watching not so much the tragedy of nineteen hundred years ago as the tragedy of their own lives and times.   Merely to dwell on the Death of Christ on Calvary would scarcely avail them more than to study the details of the assassination of Caesar at the foot of Pompey's statue. Such considerations might indeed be interesting, exciting, and even a little instructive or inspiring; but they could not be better than this, and they might be no better than morbid and harmful.

The Death of Christ, however, is unique because it is, so to say, universal. It is more than the crowning horror of all murderous histories; it is more even than the *type* of all the outrages that men have ever committed against God.   For it is just the very enactment, upon the historical stage of the world, of those repeated interior tragedies that take place in every soul that rejects or insults Him; since the God whom we crucify within is the same God that was once crucified without. There is not an exterior detail in the Gospel which may not be interiorly repeated in the spiritual life of a sinner; the process recorded by the Evangelists must be more or less identical with the process of all apostasy from God.

For, first, there is the Betrayal of Conscience, as a beginning of the tragedy; its betrayal by those elements of our nature that are intended as its friends and protectors—by Emotion or Forethought, for example. Then Conscience is led away, bound, to be judged; for there can be no mortal sin without deliberation, and no man ever yet fell into it without conducting first a sort of hasty mock-trial or two in which a sham Prudence or a false idea of Liberty solemnly decide that Conscience is in the wrong. Yet even then Conscience persists, and so He is made to appear absurd and ridiculous, and set beside the Barabbas of a coarse and sturdy lower nature that makes no high pretensions and boasts of it. And so the drama proceeds and Conscience is crucified: Conscience begins to be silent, breaking the deepening gloom now and again with protests that grow weaker every time, and at last Conscience dies indeed. And thenceforward there can be no hope, save in the miracle of Resurrection.

This Cross of Calvary, then, is not a mere type or

picture; it is a fact identical with that so dreadfully familiar to us in spiritual life. For Christ is not one Person, and Conscience something else, but it is actually Christ who speaks in Conscience and Christ, therefore, Who is crucified in mortal sin.

Let us, then, be plain with ourselves. We are watching not only Christ's Death but our own, since we are watching the Death of Christ *Who is our Life*.

THE FIRST WORD

Father forgive them, for they know not what they do.

In previous considerations we have studied the Life of Christ in His Mystical Body from an angle at which the strange and innumerable paradoxes which abound in all forms of life at a certain depth become visible. And we have seen how these paradoxes lie in those strata, so to say, where the Divinity and the Humanity meet. Christ is God and God cannot die; therefore Christ became man in order to be able to do so. The Church is Divine and therefore all-holy, but she dwells in a Body of sinful Humanity and reckons her sinners to be her children and members no less than her saints.

We will continue to regard the crucifixion of Jesus Christ and the Words which He spoke from the Cross from the same angle, and to find, therefore, the same characteristic paradoxes and mysteries in all that we see. In the First Word we meet the *Paradox of Divine Forgiveness*.

I. Ordinary human forgiveness is no more than a natural virtue, resulting from a natural sense of justice, and if a man is normal, his forgiveness will be a natural and inevitable part of the process of reconciliation so soon as a certain kind of restitution has been made. For example, a friend of mine sins against me — he injures, perhaps, my good name; and my natural answer is the emotion of resentment towards him and, perhaps, of actual revenge. But what I chiefly resent is my friend's stupidity and his ignorance of my real character. "I am angry," I say, with perfect sincerity, "not so much at the thing he has said of me, as at this proof of his incapacity to understand me. I thought he was my friend, that he was in sympathy with my character or, at least, that he understood it sufficiently to do me justice. But now, from what he has just said of me, I see that he does not. If the thing he said were true of me, the most of my anger would be gone. But I see that he does not know me, after all."

And then, presently, my friend does understand that he has wronged me; that the gossip he repeated or the construction he put upon my actions was not fair or true. And immediately that I become aware of this, from him or from another, my resentment goes, if I have any natural virtue at all; it goes because my wounded pride is healed. I forgive him easily and naturally because he knows now what he has done.

II. How entirely different from this easy, self-loving, human forgiveness is the Divine Forgiveness of Christ! Now it is true that in the conscience of Pilate, the unjust representative of Justice, and in that thing that called itself conscience in Herod, and in the hearts of the priests who denounced their God, and of the soldiers who executed their overlord, and of Judas who betrayed his friend, in all these there was surely a certain uneasiness — such an uneasiness is actually recorded of the first and the last of the list — a certain faint shadow of perception and knowledge of what it was that they had done and were doing. And, for the natural man, it would have been comparatively easy to forgive such injuries on that account. "I forgive them," such a man might have said from his cross, "because there is just a glimmer of knowledge left; there is just one spark in their hearts that still does me justice, and for the sake of that I can try, at least, to put away my resentment and ask God to forgive them."

But Jesus Christ cries, "Forgive them because they do *not* know what they do! Forgive them because they need it so terribly, since they do not even know that they need it! Forgive in them that which is unforgivable!"

III. Two obvious points present themselves in conclusion.

(1) First, it is *Divine* Forgiveness that we need, since no sinner of us all knows the full malice of sin. One man is a slave, let us say, to a sin of the flesh, and seeks to reassure himself by the reflection that he injures no one but himself; ignorant as he is of the outrage to God the Holy Ghost Whose temple he is ruining. Or a woman repeats again every piece of slanderous gossip that comes her way and comforts herself in moments of compunction by reflecting that she "means no harm"; ignorant as she is of the discouragement of souls of which she is the cause and of the seeds of distrust and enmity sown among friends. In fact it is incredible that any sinner ever *knows what it is that he does* by sin. We need, therefore, the Divine Forgiveness and not the human, the pardon that descends when we are unaware that we must have it or die; the love of the Father Who, *while we are yet a great way off, runs to meet us*, and Who teaches us for the first time, by the warmth of His welcome, the icy distances to which we had wandered. If we *knew*, anyone could forgive us. It is because we do not that only God, Who knows all things, can forgive us effectively.

(2) And it is this *Divine* Forgiveness that we ourselves have to extend to those that sin against us, since only those who so forgive can be forgiven. We must not wait until wounded pride is made whole by the conscious shame of our enemy; until the debt is paid by acknowledgment and we are complacent once more in the knowl-

edge that justice has been done to us at last. On the contrary, the only forgiveness that is supernatural, and which, therefore, alone is meritorious, is that which reaches out to men's ignorance and not their knowledge of their need.

THE SECOND WORD

Amen I say to thee, to-day thou shalt be with Me in Paradise.

Our Divine Lord, in this Second Word, immediately applies and illustrates the First and drives its lesson home. He shows us how the rain of mercy that poured out of heaven in answer to the prayer He made just now enlightens the man who, above all others present on Calvary, was the most abjectly ignorant of all; the man who, himself at the very heart of the tragedy, understood it less, probably, than the smallest child on the outskirts of the crowd.

His life had been one long defiance of the laws of both God and man. He had been a member of one of those troops of human vermin that crawl round Jerusalem, raiding solitary houses, attacking solitary travellers, guilty of sins at once the bloodiest and the meanest, comparable only to the French *apaches* of our own day. Well, he had been gripped at last by the Roman machine, caught in some sordid adventure, and here, resentful and furious and contemptuous, full of bravado and terror, he snarled like a polecat at every human face he saw, snarled and spat at the Divine Face Itself that looked at him from a cross that was like his own; and, since he had not even a spark of the honour that is reputed to exist "among thieves," taunted his "fellow criminal" for the folly of His "crime."

"If thou be the Christ, save Thyself and us."

Again, then, the Paradox is plain enough. Surely an educated priest, or a timid disciple, or a good-hearted dutiful soldier who hated the work he was at, surely one of these will be the first object of Christ's pardon; and so one of these would have been, if one of ourselves had hung there. But when God forgives, He forgives the most ignorant first — that is, the most remote from forgiveness—and makes, not Peter or Caiphas or the Centurion, but Dismas the thief, the firstfruits of Redemption.

I. The first effect of the Divine Mercy is Enlightenment. *Before they call, I will answer.* Before the thief feels the first pang of sorrow Grace is at work on him, and for the first time in his dreary life he begins to understand. And an extraordinary illumination shines in his soul. For no expert penitent after years of spirituality, no sorrowful saint, could have prayed more perfectly than this outcast. His intellect, perhaps, took in little or nothing of the great forces that were active about him and within him; he knew, perhaps, explicitly little or nothing of Who this was that hung beside him;

yet his soul's intuition pierces to the very heart of the mystery and expresses itself in a prayer that combines at once a perfect love, an exquisite humility, an entire confidence, a resolute hope, a clear-sighted faith, and an unutterable patience; his soul blossoms all in a moment: *Lord, remember me when Thou comest in Thy Kingdom.* He saw the glory behind the shame, the Eternal Throne behind the Cross, and the future behind the present; and he asked only to be *remembered* when the glory should transfigure the shame and the Cross be transformed into the Throne; for he understood what that remembrance would mean: "*Remember, Lord,* that I suffered at Thy side."

II. So perfect, then, are the dispositions formed in him by grace that at one bound *the last is first.* Not even Mary and John shall have the instant reward that shall be his; for them there are other gifts, and the first are those of separation and exile. For the moment, then, this man steps into the foremost place and they who have hung side by side on Calvary shall walk side by side to meet those waiting souls beyond the veil who will run so eagerly to welcome them. *To-day thou shalt be with Me in Paradise.*

III. Now this Paradox, *the last shall be first,* is an old doctrine of Christ, so startling and bewildering that He has been forced to repeat it again and again. He taught it in at least four parables: in the parables of *the Lost Piece of Silver, the Lost Sheep, the Prodigal Son,* and *the Vineyard.* The Nine Pieces lie neglected on the table, the Ninety-nine sheep are exiled in the Fold, the Elder Son is, he thinks, overlooked and slighted, and the Labourers complain of favouritism. Yet still, even after all this teaching, the complaint goes up from Christians that God is too loving to be quite just. A convert, perhaps, comes into the Church in middle age and in a few months develops the graces of Saint Teresa and becomes one of her daughters. A careless black-guard is condemned to death for murder and three weeks later dies upon the scaffold the death of a saint, at the very head of the line. And the complaints seem natural enough. *Thou hast made them equal unto us who have borne the burden and heat of the day.*

Yet look again, you Elder Sons. Have your religious, careful, timid lives ever exhibited anything resembling that depth of self-abjection to which the Younger Son has attained? Certainly you have been virtuous and conscientious; after all, it would be a shame if you had not been so, considering the wealth of grace you have always enjoyed. But have you ever even striven seri-ously after the one single moral quality which Christ holds up in His own character as the point of imitation: *Learn of Me, for I am meek and lowly of heart?* It is surely significant that He does not say, expressly, Learn of Me to be pure, or courageous, or fervent; but *Learn to be humble,* for in this, above all, you shall *find rest to your souls.* Instead, have you not had a kind of gentle pride in your religion or your virtue or your fastidiousness? In a word, you have not been as excellent an Elder Son as your brother has been a Younger. You have not corresponded with your graces as he has corresponded with his. You have never yet been capable of sufficient lowliness to come home (which is so much harder than to remain there), or of sufficient humility to begin for the first time to work with all your heart only an hour before sunset.

Begin, then, at the beginning, not half-way up the line. Go down to the church door and beat your breast and say not, God reward me who have done so much for Him, but *God be merciful to me* who have done so little. Get off your seat amongst the Pharisees and go down on your knees and weep behind Christ's couch, if perhaps He may at last say to you, *Friend, come up higher.*

THE THIRD WORD

Woman, behold thy son. Behold thy mother.

Our Divine Lord now turns, from the soul who at one bound has sprung into the front rank, to those two souls who have never left it, and supremely to that Mother on whose soul sin has never yet breathed, on whose breast Incarnate God had rested as inviolate and secure as on the Bosom of the Eternal Father, that Mother who was His Heaven on earth. Standing beside her is the

one human being who is least unworthy to be there,
now that Joseph has passed to his reward and John the
Baptist has gone to join the Prophets — *the disciple
whom Jesus loved*, who had lain on the breast of Jesus
as Jesus had lain on the breast of Mary.

Our Lord has just shown how He deals with His dear
sinners; now He shows how He will *be glorified with His
Saints*. The Paradox of this Word is that Death, the
divider of those who are separated from God, is the
bond of union between those that are united to
Him.

I. Death is the one inexorable enemy of human
society as constituted apart from God. A king dies
and his kingdom is at once in danger of disruption. A
child dies and his mother prays that she may bear
another, lest his father and she should drift apart.
Death is the supreme sower of discord and disunion,
then, in the natural order, since he is the one supreme
enemy of natural life. He is the noonday terror of
the Rich Fool of the parable and the nightmare of the
Poor Fool, since those who place their hope in this life
see that death is the end of their hope. For these
there is no appeal beyond the grave.

II. Now precisely the opposite of all this is true in
the supernatural order, since the gate of death, viewed
from the supernatural side, is an entrance and not an
ending, a beginning and not a close. This may be seen
to be so even in a united human family in this world,

the members of whom are living the supernatural life; for where such a family is living in the love of God, Death, when he comes, draws not only the survivors closer together, but even those whom he seems to have separated. He does not bring consternation and terror and disunion, but he awakens hope and tenderness, he smooths away old differences, he explains old misunderstandings.

Our Blessed Lord has already, over the grave of Lazarus, hinted that this shall be so, so soon as He has consecrated death by His own dying. *He that believeth in Me shall never die.* He, that is to say, who has *died with Christ*, whose centre henceforward is in the supernatural, simply no longer finds death to be what nature finds it. It no longer makes for division but for union; it no longer imperils or ends life and interest and possession, but releases them from risk and mortality.

Here, then, He deliberately and explicitly acts upon this truth. He once raised Lazarus and the daughter of Jairus and the Widow's Son from the dead, for death's sting could, at that time, be drawn in no other way; but now that He Himself is *tasting death for every man*, He performs an even more emphatically supernatural act and conquers death by submitting to it instead of by commanding it. Life had already united, so far as mortal life can unite, those two souls who loved Him and one another so well. These two, since they knew Him so perfectly, knew each the other too as perfectly as knowledge and sympathy can unite souls in this life. But now the whole is to be raised a stage higher. They had already been united on the living breast of Jesus; now, over His dead body, they were to be made yet more one.

It is marvellous that, after so long, our imaginations should still be so tormented and oppressed by the thought of death; that we should still be so *without understanding* that we think it morbid to be in love with death, for it is far more morbid to be in fear of it. It is not that our reason or our faith are at fault; it is only that that most active and untamable faculty of ours, which we call imagination, has not yet assimilated the truth, accepted by both our faith and our reason, that for those who are in the friendship of God death is simply not that at all which it is to others. It does not, as has been said, end our lives or our interests; on the contrary it liberates and fulfils them.

And all this it does because Jesus Christ has Himself plunged into the heart of Death and put out his fires. Henceforth we are one family in Him if we do His will— *his brother and sister and mother;* and Mary is our Mother, not by nature, which is accidental, but by supernature, which is essential.   Mary is my Mother and John is my brother, since, if I have died with Christ, it *is no longer I that live, but Christ that liveth in me.* In a word, it is the Communion of Saints which He inaugurates by this utterance and seals by His dying.

THE FOURTH WORD

My God, My God, why hast Thou forsaken Me?

Our Blessed Lord in the revelation He makes from the Cross passes gradually inwards to Himself Who is its centre. He begins in the outermost circle of all, with the ignorant sinners. He next deals with the one sinner who ceased to be ignorant, and next with those who were always nearest to Himself, and now at last He reveals the deepest secret of all. This is the central Word of the Seven in every sense. There is no need to draw attention to the Paradox it expresses.

I. First, then, let us remind ourselves of the revealed dogma that Jesus Christ was the Eternal Son of the Father; that He dwelt always in the Bosom of that Father; that when He left heaven He *did not leave the Father's side;* that at Bethlehem and Nazareth and Galilee and Jerusalem and Gethsemane and Calvary He was always the *Word that was with God* and *the Word* that *was God.* Next, that the eyes even of His Sacred Humanity looked always and continuously upon the Face of God, since His union with God was entire and complete: as He looked up into His Mother's face from the manger, He saw behind it the Face of His Father; as He cried in Gethsemane, *If it be possible,* even in His Sacred Humanity He knew that it could not be; as He groaned out on Calvary that God had forsaken Him, He yet looked without one instant's intermission into the glory of heaven and saw His Father there.

Yet simultaneously with these truths it is also true that His cry of dereliction was incalculably more of a reality than when first uttered by David or, since, by any desolate sinner in the thickest spiritual darkness. All the miseries of holy and sinful souls, heaped together, could not approach even afar off the intolerable misery of Christ. For of His own will He refused to be consoled at all by that Presence which He could never lack, and of His own will He chose to be pierced and saturated and tormented by the sorrow He could never deserve. He held firm against the touch of consolation every power of His Divine and Human Being and, simultaneously, flung them open to the assaults of every pain. And if the psychology of this state is altogether beyond our power to understand, we may remind ourselves that it is the psychology of the *Word made Flesh* that is confronting us. . . . Do we expect to understand that? . . .

II. There is a human phrase, however, itself a paradox, yet corresponding to something which we know to be true, which throws some faint glimmer of light upon this impenetrable darkness and seems to extend Christ's experience upon the Cross so as to touch our own human life. It is a phrase that describes a condition well known to spiritual persons: "To leave God for God."

(1) The simplest and lowest form of this state is that condition in which we acquiesce with our will in the withdrawal of ordinary spiritual consolation. Certainly it is an inexplicable state, since both the ordinary aids to our will — our understanding and our emotion — are, by the very nature of the case, useless to it. Our heart revolts from that dereliction and our understanding fails to comprehend the reasons for it. Yet we acquiesce, or at least perceive that we ought to do so; and that by doing so — by ceasing, that is, to grasp God's Presence any longer — we find it as never before. We leave God in order to find Him.

(2) The second state is that in which we find ourselves when not only do all consolations leave us, but the very grip of intelligent faith goes too; when the very reasons for faithfulness appear to vanish. It is an incalculably more bitter trial, and soul after soul fails under it and must be comforted again by God in less august ways or perish altogether. And yet this is not the extremest pitch even of human desolation.

(3) For there is a third of which the saints tell us in broken words and images. . . .

III. Our final point, for application to ourselves, is that dereliction in some form or another is as much a stage in spiritual progress as autumn and winter are seasons of the year. The beginners have to suffer one degree, the illuminated another, and those that have approached a real Union with God a third. But all must suffer it, and each in his own degree, or progress is impossible.

Let us take courage therefore and face it, in the light of this Word. For, as we can sanctify bodily pain by the memory of the nails, so too can we sanctify spiritual pain by the memory of this darkness. If He Who *never left the Father's side* can suffer this in an unique and supreme sense, how much more should we be content to suffer it in lower degrees, who have so continually, since we came to the age of reason, been leaving not His side only, but His very house.

THE FIFTH WORD

I thirst.

Our Lord continues to reveal His own condition, since He, after all, is the key to all Humanity. If we understand anything of Him, simultaneously we shall understand ourselves far better.

He has shown us that He can truly be deprived of spiritual consolation; and the value of this deprivation; now He shows us the value of bodily deprivation also. And the Paradox for our consideration is that the Source of all can lose all; that the Creator needs His creation; that He Who offers us the *water springing up into Life Eternal* can lack the water of human life — the simplest element of all. In His Divine Dereliction He yet continues to be Human.

I. It is very usual, under this Word, to meditate on Christ's thirst for souls; and this is, of course, a legitimate thought, since it is true that His whole Being, and not merely one part of it, longed and panted on the Cross for every object of His desire. Certainly He desired souls! When does He not?

But it is easy to lose the proportion of truth, if we spiritualize everything, and pass over, as if unworthy of consideration, His bodily pain. For this Thirst of the Crucified is the final sum of all the pains of crucifixion: the physical agony, the fever produced by it, the torrential sweat, the burning of the sun — all these culminated in the torment of which this Cry is His expression.

Bodily pain, then, since Jesus not only deigned to suffer it, but to speak of it, is as much a part of the Divine process as the most spiritual of derelictions: it is an intense and a vital reality in life. It is the fashion, at present, to pose as if we were superior to such things; as if either it were too coarse for our high natures or even actually in itself evil. The truth is that we are terrified of its reality and its sting, and seek, therefore, to evade it by every means in our power. We affect to smile at the old penances of the saints and ascetics as if we ourselves had risen into a higher state of development and needed no longer such elementary aids to piety!

Let this Word, then, bring us back to our senses and

to the due proportions of truth. We are body as well as soul; we are incomplete without the body. The soul is insufficient to itself, the body has as real a part to play in Redemption as the soul which is its inmate and should be its mistress. We look for the *redemption of our body* and the *Resurrection of the Flesh*, we merit or demerit before God in our soul for the deeds done in our body.

So was it too with our Lord of His infinite compassion. The *Word was made Flesh*, dwelt in the Flesh, has assumed that Flesh into heaven. Further, He suffered in the Flesh and deigned to tell us so; and that He found that suffering all but intolerable.

II. In a well-known book a Catholic poet [1] describes with a great deal of power the development of men's nervous systems in these later days, and warns his readers against a scrupulous terror lest they, who no longer scourge themselves with briers, should be neglecting a means of sanctification. He points out, with perfect justice, that men, in these days, suffer instead in more subtle manners than did those of the Middle Ages, yet none the less physical; and puts us on our guard lest we should afflict ourselves too much. Yet we must take care, also, that we do not fall into the opposite extreme and come to regard bodily pain, (as has been said) as if it were altogether too elementary for our refined natures and as if it must have no place in

[1] Health and Holiness by Francis Thompson.

the alchemy of the spirit. This would be both dangerous and false. *What God hath joined together, let no man
put asunder!* For, if we once treat body and soul as ill-
matched companions and seek to deal with them apart,
instantly the door is flung open to the old Gnostic
horrors of sensualism on the one side or inhuman mutilation or neglect on the other.

The Church, on the other hand, is very clear and
insistent that body and soul make one man as fully as
God and Man make one Christ; and she illustrates and
directs these strange co-relations and mutual effects of
these two partners by her steady insistence on such
things as Fasting and Abstinence. And the saints are
equally clear and insistent. There never yet has been a
single soul whom the Church has raised to her altars in
whose life bodily austerity in some form has not played
a considerable part. It is true that some have warned
us against excess; but what warnings and what excess!
"Be moderate," advises St. Ignatius, that most reasonable and moderate of all the saints. "Take care that
you do not break any bones with your iron scourge.
God does not wish that!"

Pain, then, has a real place in our progress. Who
that has suffered can ever doubt it again?

Let us consider, therefore, under this Word of Christ,
whether our attitude to bodily pain is what God would
have it to be. There are two mistakes that we may be
committing. Either we may fear it too little — meet it,

that is to say, with Pagan stoicism instead of with Christianity—or we may fear it too much. *Despise not the chastening*, on one side, *or faint* on the other. It is surely the second warning that is most needed now. For pain had a real place in Christ's programme of life. He fasted for forty days at the beginning of His Ministry, and He willed every shocking detail of the Praetorium and Calvary at the end. He told us that *His Spirit willed it* and, yet more kindly, that *His Flesh was weak.* He revealed, then, that He really suffered and that He willed it so. . . . *I thirst.*

THE SIXTH WORD

It is consummated.

He has finished *His Father's business*, He has dealt with sinners and saints, and has finally disclosed to us the secrets of the Soul and the Body of His that are the hope of both sinners and saints alike. And there is no more for Him to do.

An entirely new Beginning, then, is at hand, now that the Last Sabbath is come—the Last Sabbath, so much greater than the First as Redemption is greater than Creation. For Creation is a mere introduction to the Book of Life; it is the arrangement of materials that are to be thrown instantly into confusion again by man, who should be its crown and master. The Old Testament is one medley of mistakes and fragments and broken promises and violated treaties, to reach its climax in the capital Mistake of Calvary, when men indeed *knew not what they did*. And even God Himself in the New Testament, as man in the Old, has gone down in the catastrophe and hangs here mutilated and broken. Real life, then, is now to begin.

Yet, strangely enough, He calls it an End rather than a Beginning. *Consummatum est!*

I. The one and only thing in human life that God desires to end is Sin. There is not a pure joy or a sweet human relationship or a selfless ambition or a divine hope which He does not desire to continue and to be crowned and transfigured beyond all ambition and all hope. On the contrary, He desires only to end that one single thing which ruins relationships and spoils joy and poisons aspirations. For up to the present there is not one page of history which has not this blot upon it.

God has had to tolerate, for lack of better, such miserable specimens of humanity! *Jacob have I loved!* . . . *David a man after my heart;* the one a poor, mean, calculating man, who had, however, that single glimmer of the supernatural which Esau, for all his genial sturdiness, was without; the other an adulterous murderer, who yet had grace enough for real contrition. Hitherto He has been content with so little. He has accepted vinegar for want of wine.

Next, God has had to tolerate, and indeed to sanction —such an unworthy worship of Himself—all the blood of the temple and the spilled entrails and the nameless horrors. And yet this was all to which men could rise; for without it, they never could have learned the more nameless horror of sin.

Last, for His worshippers He has had to content Himself with but one People instead of *all peoples and nations and languages*. And what a People, — whom even Moses could not bear for their treachery and instability! And all this wretched record ends in the Crime of Calvary, at which the very earth revolts and the sun grows dark with shame. Is it any wonder that Christ cried, Thank God that is all done with at last!

II. Instead of this miserable past, then, what is to come? What is that *New Wine He would drink with us in His Father's Kingdom?* First; real and complete saints of God are to take the place of the fragmentary saints of the Old Dispensation, saints with heads of gold and feet of clay. Souls are to be born again in Baptism, not merely sealed by circumcision, and to be purified before they can contract any actual guilt of their own. And, of these, many shall keep their baptismal innocence and shall go, wearing that white robe, before God Who gave it them. Others again shall lose it, but regain it once more, and, through the power of the Precious Blood, shall rise to heights of which Jacob and David never even dreamed. To *awake in His likeness* was the highest ambition of *the man after God's Heart;* but to be not merely like Christ, but one with Him, is the hope of the Christian. *I live,* the new saints shall say with truth, *yet now not I, but Christ liveth in me.*

Next, instead of the old worship of blood and pain there shall be an Unbloody Sacrifice and a *Pure Offering* in which shall be all the power and propitiation of Calvary without its pain, all the glory without the degradation. And last, in place of the old enclosed Race of Israel shall be a Church of all nations and tongues, one vast Society, with all walls thrown down and all divisions done away, one Jerusalem from above, that shall be the Mother of us all.

III. That, then, is what Christ intended as He cried, *It is consummated.* Behold *the old things are passed away!* Behold, *I make all things new!*

And now let us see how far that is fulfilled. Where is there, in me, the New Wine of the Gospel?

I have all that God can give me from His Throne on Calvary. I have the truth that He proclaimed and the grace that He released. Yet is there in me, up to the present, even one glimmer of what is meant by Sanctity? Am I even within an appreciable distance of the saints who knew not Christ? Have I ever wrestled like Jacob or wept like David? Has my religion, that is to say, ever inspired me beyond the low elevation of joy into the august altitudes of pain? Is it possible that with me the old is not put away, the *old man* is not yet dead, and the *new man* not yet *put on?* Is that New Sacrifice the light of my daily life? Have I done anything except hinder the growth of Christ's Church, anything except drag down her standards, so far as I am able, to my own low level? Is there a single soul now in the world who owes, under God, her conversion to my efforts?

Why, as I watch my life and review it in His Presence it would seem as if I had done nothing but disappoint Him all my days! He cried, like the deacon of His own Sacrifice, Go! it is done! *Ite; missa est!* The Sacrifice is finished here; go out in its strength to live the life which it makes possible!

Let me at least begin to-day, have done with my old compromises and shifts and evasions. *Ite; missa est!*

THE SEVENTH WORD

Father, into Thy hands I commend My spirit.

He has cried with a loud voice, and the rocks have rent to its echo, and the earth is shaken, and the Veil of the Old Testament is torn from top to bottom as the Old Covenant passes into the New and the enclosed sanctity of the Most Holy Place breaks out into the world. And now, as the level sun shines out again beneath the pall of clouds, He whispers, as at Mary's knee in Nazareth, the old childish prayer and yields up His spirit into His Father's hands.

The last Paradox, then, is uttered. He Who saves others cannot save Himself! The Shepherd of souls relinquishes His own. For, as we cannot save our lives unless we lose them for His sake, so He too cannot save them unless He loses His for our sake.

I. This, then, is merely the summary of all that has gone before; it is the word *Finis* written at the end of this new Book of Life which He has written in His Blood. It is the silence of the white space at the close of the last page. Yet it is, too, the final act that gives value to all that have preceded it. If Christ had not died, our faith would be vain.

Oh! these New Theologies that see in Christ's Death merely the end of His Life! Why, it is the very point and climax of His Life that He should lay it down! Like Samson himself, that strange prototype of the Strong Man armed, he slew more of the enemies of our souls by His Death than by all His gracious Life. *For this cause He came into the world.* For Sacrifice, which is the very heart of man's instinctive worship of God, was set there, imperishably, in order to witness to and be ratified by His One Offering which alone could truly take away sins; and to deny it or to obscure it is to deny or to obscure the whole history of the human race, from the Death of Abel to the Death of Christ, to deny or obscure the significance of every lamb that bled in the Temple and of every wine-offering poured out before the Holy Place, to deny or to obscure (if we will but penetrate to the roots of things) the free will of Man and the Love of God. If Christ had not died, our faith would be vain.

II. Once again, then, let us turn to the event in our own lives that closes them; that death which, united to Christ's, is our entrance into liberty and, disunited, the supreme horror of existence.

(1) For without Christ death is a violent interruption to life, introducing us to a new existence of which we know nothing, or to no existence at all. Without Christ, however great our hopes, it is abrupt, appalling, stunning, and shattering. It is this at the best, and, at the worst, it is peaceful only as the death of a beast is peaceful.

(2) Yet, with Christ, it is harmonious and continuous with all that has gone before, since it is the final movement of a life that is already *dead with Christ*, the last stage of a process of mortality, and the stage that ends its pain. It is just one more passing phase, by which is changed the key of that music that every holy life makes always before God.

There is, then, the choice. We may, if we will, die fighting to the end a force that must conquer us however we may fight, resisting the irresistible. Or we may die, in lethargic resignation, as dogs die, without hopes or regrets, since the past, without Christ, is as meaningless as the future. Or we may die, like Christ, and with Him, yielding up a spirit that came from the Father back again into His Fatherly hands, content that He Who brought us into the world should receive us when we go out again, confident that, as the thread of His purpose is plain in earthly life, it shall shine yet more plainly in the life beyond.

One last look, then, at Jesus shows us the lines smoothed from His face and the agony washed from His eyes. May our souls and the souls of all the faithful departed, through His Mercy, rest in Him!

XI
LIFE AND DEATH

LIFE AND DEATH

As dying, and behold we live. — II COR. VI. 9.

WE have considered, so far, a number of paradoxical phenomena exhibited in the life of Catholicism and have attempted to find their reconciliation in the fact that the Catholic Church is at once Human and Divine. In her striving, for example, after a Divine and supernatural Peace, of which she alone possesses the secret, she *resists even unto blood* all human attempts to supplant this by another. As a human society, again, she avails herself freely of human opportunities and aids, of earthly and created beauty, for the setting forth of her message; yet she can survive, as can no human society, when she is deprived of her human rights and her acquired wealth. As human she numbers the great multitude of the world's sinners among her children, yet as Divine she has produced the saints. As Divine she bases all her gospel on a Revelation which can be apprehended only by Faith, yet as human she employs the keenest and most profound intellects for its analysis and its propagation. In these and in many other similar points it has been attempted to show why she offers now one aspect and now another to human criticism, and how it is that the very charges made against her become, when viewed in the light of her double claim, actual credentials and arguments on behalf of that claim. Finally, in the meditations upon the *Seven Words* of Christ, we considered very briefly how, in the hours of the deepest humiliation of His Humanity, He revealed again and again the characteristics of His Divinity.

It now remains to consider that point in which she most manifests that double nature of hers and, simultaneously therefore, presents, as in a kind of climax, her identity, under human terms, with Him Who, Himself the Lord of Life, conquered death by submitting to it and, by His Resurrection from the dead, showed Himself *the Son of God with power*.

I. Death, the world tells us, is the final end of all things, and is the one universal law of which evasion is impossible; and this is true, not of the individual only, but of society, of nations, of civilization, and even, it would seem, ultimately of physical life itself. Every vital energy therefore that we possess can be directed not to the abolition, but only to the postponement of this final full close to which the most ecstatic created harmony must come at last.

Our physicians cannot heal us, they can merely ward off death for a little. Our statesmen cannot establish an eternal federation, they can but help to hold a crumbling society together for a little longer. Our civilization cannot really evolve an immortal superman, it can but render ordinary humanity a little less mortal, temporarily and in outward appearance. Death, then, in the world's opinion, is the duellist who is bound to win. We may parry, evade, leap aside for a little; we may even advance upon him and seem to threaten his very existence; our energies, in fact, must be concentrated upon this conflict if we are to survive at all. But it is only in seeming, at the best. The moment must come when, driven back to the last barrier, our last defence falters . . . and Death has only to wipe his sword.

Now the attitude of the Catholic Church towards Death is not only the most violent reversal of the world's policy, but the most paradoxical, too, of all her methods. For, while the world attempts to keep Death at arm's length, the Church strives to embrace him. Where the world draws his sword to meet Death's assault, the Church spreads her heart only to receive it. She is in love with Death, she pursues him, honours him, extols Him. She places over her altars not a Risen Christ, but a dying One.

If thou wilt be perfect, she cries to the individual soul, *give up all that thou hast and follow me.* "Give up all that makes life worth living, strip thyself of every advantage that sustains thy life, of all that makes thee effective." It is this that is her supreme appeal, not indeed uttered, with all its corollaries, to all her children, but to those only that desire perfection. Yet to all, in a sense, the appeal is there. *Die daily*, die to self, mortify, yield, give in. *If any man will save his life, he must lose it.*

So too, in her dealings with society, is her policy judged suicidal by a world that is in love with its own kind of life. It is suicidal, cries that world, to relinquish in France all on which the temporal life of the Church depends; for how can that society survive which renounces the very means of existence? It is suicidal to demand the virgin life of the noblest of her children, suicidal to desert the monarchical cause of one country, and to set herself in opposition to the Republican ideals of another. For even she, after all, is human and must conform to human conditions. Even she, however august her claims, must make terms with the world if she desires to live in it.

And this comment has been made upon her actions in every age. She condemned Arius, when a little compromise might surely have been found; and lost half her children. She condemned Luther and lost Germany; Elizabeth, and lost England. At every crisis she has made the wrong choice, she has yielded when she should have resisted, resisted when she should have yielded. The wonder is that she survives at all.

Yes, that is the wonder. *As dying, behold she lives!*

II. The answer of course is easy. It is that she

simply does not desire the kind of life which the world reckons alone to be life. To her that is not life at all. She desires of course to survive as a human society, and she is assured that she always shall so survive. Yet it is not on the ordinary terms of ordinary society that she desires survival. It is not a *natural* life of which she is ambitious, a life that draws its strength from human conditions and human environment, a life, therefore, that waxes and wanes with those human conditions and ultimately meets their fate, but a *supernatural* life that draws its strength from God. And she recognizes, as one of the most fundamental paradoxes of all, that such a life can be gained and held only through what the world calls "death."

She does not, then, want merely the life of a prosperous human state, whether monarchy or republic. There are times indeed in her history when such an accompaniment to her real existence is useful to her effectiveness; and she has, of course, the right, as have other societies, to earthly dominions that may have been won and presented to her by her children. Or through her ministers, as in Paraguay, she may administer for a while the ordinary civil affairs of men who choose to be loyal to her government. Yet if, for one instant, such a responsibility were really to threaten her spiritual effectiveness—if, that is, the choice were really presented to her between spiritual and temporal dominion — she would let all the kingdoms of the world go in an instant, to retain her kingdom from God; she would gladly *suffer the loss of all things* to retain Christ.

And how is it possible to deny for one instant that her success has been startling and overwhelming — this fructification of Life by Death.

Are there any human beings, for example, who have been more effective and influential than her saints — men and women, that is to say, who have *died daily*, in order to live indeed? They have not, it is true, prospered, let us say, as business men, directors of companies, or government officials, but such a success is simply not her ideal for them, not their own ideal for themselves. That is precisely the kind of life to which they have, as a rule, determinedly and perseveringly died. Yet their effectiveness in this world has been none the less. Are any kings remembered as is the beggar Labré who gnawed cabbage stalks in the gutters of Rome? Are the names of any statesmen of, let us say, even a hundred years ago, reverenced and repeated as is the name of the woman of Spain called Teresa of Jesus who, four hundred years ago, ruled a few nuns within the enclosure of a convent? Are any musicians or artists loved to-day with such rapture as is God's little troubadour, called Francis, who made music for himself and the angels by rubbing one stick across another?

Or, again, is any empire that the world has ever seen

so great, so loyally united in itself, so universal and yet
so rigorous as is that spiritual empire whose capital is
Rome? Is there any nation with so fierce a patriotism
as she who is Supernational? Earthly kings speak from
their thrones and what happens? And an old man in
Rome who wears three crowns on his head speaks
from his prison in the Vatican and all the earth rings
with it.

Has her policy, then, been so suicidal after all? From
the world's point of view it has never been anything else.
Her history is but one long example of the sacrifice of
human activities and earthly opportunities; she has
expelled from her pulpits the most brilliant of her
children, she has silenced or alienated the most eloquent
of her defenders. She has cut off from herself all that
she should have kept, and hugged to her arms all that
she should have relinquished! She has never done anything but die! She never does anything but live!

III. Turn, then, to the life of her Lord for the solution
of this riddle. Last week[1] He was going to His Death.
He was losing, little by little, all that bound Him to Life.
The multitudes that had followed Him hitherto were
leaving Him by units and groups, they who might have
formed His armies to seat Him on the throne of His father
David. Disloyalty had made its way even among His
chosen body-guard, and already Judas is bargaining for

[1] This Sermon was preached on Easter Day.

the price of His Master's blood. Even the most loyal of all are dismayed, and presently will *forsake Him and flee* when the swords flash out in the garden of Gethsemane. A few weeks ago in Galilee thousands were leaving Him for the last time; and when, once again, a company seemed to rally, He wept! And so at last the sacrifice was complete and, one by one, He laid down of His own will every tie that kept Him in life. And then on Good Friday itself He suffered that beauty of His *Face to be marred* so that no man would ever *desire Him* any more, silenced the melody of the Voice that had broken so many hearts and made them whole again; He stretched out His Shepherd's Hands with which alone He could gather His sheep to His Breast, and the Feet that alone could bear Him into the wilderness to *seek after that which was lost*. Was there ever a Suicide such as this, such a despair of high hopes, such a ruin of all ambition, a dying so complete and irremediable as the Dying of Jesus Christ?

And now on Easter Day look at Him again and see how He lives as never before. See how the Life that has been His for thirty years — the Life of God made Man—itself pales almost to a phantom before the glory of that same Life transfigured by Death. Three days ago He fainted beneath the scourge and nails; now He shows the very scars of His Passion to be the emblems of immortal strength. Three days ago He spoke in human words to those only that were near Him, and limited Himself under human terms of space and time; He speaks now in every heart. Three days ago He gave His Body to the few who knelt at His Table; to-day in ten thousand tabernacles that same Body may be worshipped by all who come.

In a word, He has exchanged a Natural Life for a Supernatural in every plane at once. He has laid down the Natural Life of His Body to take it back again supernaturalized for ever. He has died that His Life may be released; He has *finished* in order to begin.

It is easy, then, to see why it is that the Church *dies daily*, why it is that she is content to be stripped of all that makes her life effective, why she too permits her hands to be bound and her feet fettered and her beauty marred and her voice silenced so far as men can do those things. She is human? Yes; she dwells in a *body that is prepared* for her, but prepared chiefly that she may suffer in it. Her far-reaching hands are not hers merely that she may bind up with them the broken-hearted, nor her swift feet hers merely that she may run on them to succour the perishing, nor her head and heart hers merely that she may ponder and love. But all this sensitive human organism is hers that at last she may agonize in it, bleed from it from a thousand wounds, be lifted up in it to draw all men to her cross.

She does not desire, then, in this world, the *throne of*

her Father David, nor the kind of triumph which is the only kind that the world understands to be so. She desires one life and one triumph only—the Risen Life of her Saviour. And this, at last, is the transfiguration of her Humanity by the power of her Divinity and the vindication of them both.